Concepción Picciotto (1936–2016)

An Hachette UK Company
www.hachette.co.uk

First published in Great Britain in 2018 by
Cassell Illustrated, a division of
Octopus Publishing Group Ltd
Carmelite House
50 Victoria Embankment
London EC4Y 0DZ
www.octopusbooks.co.uk

Distributed in the US by Hachette Book Group
1290 Avenue of the Americas
4th and 5th Floors
New York, NY 10104

Distributed in Canada by Canadian Manda Group
664 Annette St.
Toronto, Ontario, Canada M6S 2C8

ISBN 978 1 78840 041 1

Printed and bound in China
10 9 8 7 6 5 4 3 2 1

Commissioning Editor Romilly Morgan
Senior Editor Pauline Bache
Copy Editor Alison Wormleighton
Assistant Editor Ellie Corbett
Art Director and Designer Yasia Williams-Leedham
Illustrators Allegra Lockstadt, Sara Netherway, Lauren Simkin Berke, Hannah Berman, María Hergueta, Miriam Castillo, Marcela Quiroz, Shreyas Krishnan, Laura Inksetter, Tanya Heidrich, W T Frick, Hélène Baum, Grace Helmer
Production Controller Meskerem Berhane

Forgotten Women

The Leaders

ZING TSJENG

Contents

everyone knows a forgotten woman. I'm talking about the women that we hold dear in our hearts; the ones we raise in conversation over a drink or two. You know, the ones whose names are usually met with a look of surprise, a furrowed brow and the cry, "Oh, I've never heard of her before – how weird!"

The truth is, it is far more likely that women have been forgotten than men. All you need to do is look at the last two thousand years for proof: the history books are awash with dudes in togas or academic dress, pontificating on subjects like science, literature and politics. When women do make a brief appearance, they're contextualized by their gender: here's the female Socrates! Put it this way: you never hear about the male Joan of Arc...

Women only occupy around a half a per cent of recorded history. They did pretty well in the 35,000 years preceding the birth of Christ: nine out of ten of all discovered archeological figures from that time have been female. Then, like a wisp of smoke, women began to wither away in the public record. They appear less and less, or are memorable only for their feminine wiles and their sexuality.

Given that the fairer sex makes up about half of the world's population at any given moment, it begs the question: what on earth were they doing? As it turns out, women were toiling, researching, exploring and fighting for their place in the world. They were in combat on the battle lines, making

earth-shattering discoveries and actively participating in the great revolutions – intellectual, scientific and sociopolitical – of their respective centuries. In fact, women were doing all of the above on top of battling the sexism and prejudice that they encountered.

Growing up, I read about men like Christopher Columbus and Henry VIII, even though I was in Singapore, a country some ten thousand kilometres (six thousand miles) from Italy and England respectively. This had the unfortunate effect of making a precocious 12-year-old like me believe that fame and power were things that naturally came to white men in the West, and that the greatest achievement a woman could attain was to be an Anne of Cleves type – a wife clever enough to evade her husband's executioner. (I said I was precocious; I never said that I was smart.)

As I grew older, of course, I learned that political bravery and leadership are not the sole preserve of men. But still, contemporary politics has not been known for its gender equality. In the UK, where I now live, only 30 per cent of Members of Parliament are women, and the country ranks a measly 48th in terms of parliamentary equality. It's enough to make some slimeballs argue that women may simply be unsuited to the halls of power – in which case I suggest a quick glance at the life of Töregene Khatun, who usurped Genghis Khan's son to become the Mongol Empire's mightiest empress; or that of Eleanor of Aquitaine, whose vice-like grip on power saw her change the course of European history. I also learned that power doesn't just consist of Tudor crowns, thrones and political might; it can also come from the so-called "unwashed" masses, who demand a better and more equal society, in which the people, of all ethnicities and gender identities, have a voice. Around the world, women have been at the front lines of these movements, leading by example – from Lillian Ngoyi in the fight to end South African apartheid to Sylvia Rivera in the continuing struggle for transgender rights in the US.

Understandably, I was extremely nervous when I began writing the *Forgotten Women* series. Even with the help of The New Historia, selecting women to go into *The Leaders* presented an exquisite, if deeply pleasurable, nightmare – I wanted the book to be as diverse and representative as possible, and I had all of history from which to choose. Who to pick and who to leave out? Even the gesture of omission suggested a kind of snub or implicit criticism. In the end, I had to selfishly go with the women whose stories I myself, as that precocious 12-year-old girl, would have liked to read about – women whose stories made me nod in respect or gasp with shock. Women whose stories thrilled me, even if I disagreed with their methods. (Töregene's preferred method of execution – stuffing someone's mouth with pebbles until they suffocated – comes to mind.)

Then came another worry: who was I to decide that these were the people who merited the world's attention? Who was I to decide that they had been forgotten at all? In some cases, these women had circulated in and out of public consciousness for years. Zenobia, the queen of Palmyra, in present-day Syria, for instance, had been the subject of Chaucer's epic verse and was once the go-to inspiration for the dressing-up costumes of 19th-century British socialites. Similarly, Shirley Chisholm, the first black woman to run for the US presidency, had largely faded out of public memory before interest in her legacy was revived by Barack Obama's White House run and Hillary Clinton's subsequent candidacy.

Others here are already well known within their own countries of origin. Schoolchildren in the Dominican Republic now read about Patria, Minerva and María Teresa Mirabal, the sisters who defied the Dominican Republic's dictator Rafael Trujillo; Trujillo's obelisk on the seaside promenade of Santo Domingo is covered with a mural of the three activists. Halfway around the world, Vietnamese people continue to burn incense on the sixth day of the lunar month to remember the Trung sisters, two first-century AD military leaders who rebelled against the ruling Chinese dynasty – and I'm fairly sure that the people of the Dominican Republic and Vietnam alike would laugh at any suggestion that their national heroes have been consigned to oblivion.

Then there are those who have passed into pop culture myth, like one of my personal favourites: Ching Shih, a Chinese prostitute turned pirate queen, who left the floating brothels of Canton to command a thousands-strong seafaring army, and who inspired a brief cameo in the *Pirates of the Caribbean* franchise. So she wasn't exactly forgotten, but she wasn't quite remembered as she was – I doubt that many of us would like to be commemorated for life in a critically panned Disney film starring Johnny Depp, a white man from Kentucky in dreadlocks.

Still, I kept coming back to the idea of memory, and what a tricky beast it can be. I forget things as quickly as a goldfish forgets the sides of its fishbowl; I would forget my own shoes if they weren't usually on my feet. Forgetting is as natural to me as falling, while remembering requires active effort.

I may be an extreme case, but I suspect that history works the same way. If a woman can be forgotten once, it's fair to assume she could be forgotten again. (This is, presumably, why so many men in history have been determined to build as many outsized monuments to themselves as possible – it is significantly harder to tear down a marble statue welded to a plinth than it is to lose track of a history book.) It isn't enough to shine a light on women once – we have to do so again and again, hoping against hope that something sticks this time around and knowing that it may very well not. It is the act that matters, because it is the act of remembering that gives a name power.

This book is not the first to profile women in this way, and it won't be the last. It stands on the shoulders of historians and writers – many of them female – who have done the heavy lifting of excavating these women from the past. When you read *Forgotten Women: The Leaders*, I hope that you take it not as the concluding note on its subjects, but as a beginning – an invitation for you to begin looking deeper into their stories, and those of other women.

There are hundreds of women out there, and thousands whose names are even yet to be uncovered. Their achievements span the breadth and depth of the arts and sciences, but you can detect certain unifying threads in their lives: tenacity, bravery, ingenuity and a certain enthusiasm for saying "f*** you" to the system – or rather, a refusal to accept the hand that they have been dealt.

Sometimes, these heroes exist even closer to home. I'll bet there are even a few in your family tree who succeeded in thwarting the rules. There are millions of forgotten women. Who is yours?

The Rebels

n the 19th century, Cuba was every bit the booming, prosperous Spanish colony. But its wealth had a dark side – it flourished off the backs of thousands of slaves who worked on its plantations and in its sugar mills. By 1841, for the first time in Cuba's history, a population census revealed that there were more slaves than white residents. Out of one million people, there were 436,000 slaves, 153,000 free people of colour and just 418,000 whites[1]. The implications of the census were keenly felt among the Spanish authorities, who began to sense that the days of their grip on power – demographically, at least – were numbered.

In 1843 this division was brought into stark relief. Black slaves, as well as free people of colour and even some white Cubans, began to sorely resent Spanish rule over the island – which was especially galling when Cuba did not even have political representation in Madrid. In November, what became known as Cuba's largest countryside uprising took place, thanks to an African slave called **Carlota Lucumí** (unknown–1844)

Not much is known about Carlota; as with many slaves, her true identity was stripped from her as she made the transatlantic crossing to the New World. But her last name may give some indication of her past: Lucumí was the name given to Cuban slaves who spoke the Yoruba language of West Africa. Yoruba women, from what is now Nigeria, are known to have led troops into battle; some historians believe that Carlota may have been of noble birth and therefore familiar with matters of military planning. This helps explain her fearlessness and skill at moulding her ragtag group of rebel slaves into a fearsome army.

Rebellion had been brewing on the island since March that year. Near the port city of Cárdenas, some 116km (72 miles) east of Havana, slaves at a sugar mill killed three workers and razed buildings to the ground. Travelling along the railway tracks to neighbouring plantations, they recruited other slaves and workers to their cause. In response, the Spanish government sent soldiers and bloodhounds after them. Many were shot or hanged – but the sudden outburst of violence and the subsequent repression lit a fuse across the surrounding countryside of Matanzas province. That summer, the air was filled with the pounding sound of slaves playing the traditional talking drums, urging others to join them in revolt.

Carlota was one slave who answered the call. Fermina, an enslaved woman from the nearby Acana sugar estate, had been imprisoned two months earlier for plotting rebellion. Carlota joined a group of other slaves to free Fermina, and she led an uprising at both the Acana mill and another plantation, the Triunvirato sugar estate. The slaves killed their overseers, took their weapons and set buildings ablaze. Ruthless and vengeful, Carlota took no prisoners. Later, one of her targets – the Triunvirato overseer's daughter – spoke of her terror during the attack, saying that Carlota wounded her with a pruning machete and only fell back when her male companions told her that her victim was probably already dead. In March 1944, at some point during the uprising, Carlota was struck down; her body was found the following morning.

The Spanish colonial authorities were vicious in their crackdown. In the wake of the uprising, thousands of black people around Matanzas – slaves and free people of colour alike – were taken into custody. Many were lashed and tortured to death without trial; one American visitor, Dr John Wurdemann, described "slaughterhouses", in which "a thousand lashes" would be inflicted on a single victim to "extort confessions".[2]

But Carlota had the last laugh. Less than half a century later, slavery was finally abolished in Cuba, and she emerged as a Cuban symbol of freedom and resistance against colonial oppression. Today, in the grounds of the ruined Triunvirato mill, there stands a statue of Carlota, holding a machete in her hand.

race O'Malley (1530–1603) called it "maintenance by land and sea", but others disagreed with this 16th-century Irishwoman's euphemistic framing of her profession. After all, piracy – and fearsome, bloodthirsty piracy at that – was piracy.

Known variously as Granuaile, Gráinne Ní Mháille or Gráinne Mhaol, the pirate queen was labelled by her English adversaries "a director of thieves and murderers at sea"[3] and a "woman who hath imprudently passed the part of womanhood"[4]. As Tudor England attempted to conquer and control Ireland, and native clans feuded among themselves, Grace's ultimate triumph was to rise above internecine conflict and secure the survival of herself and her family.

Born to a seafaring chieftain who ruled what is now part of County Mayo in the Irish province of Connaught, Grace was married off at 16 but was never going to be satisfied with domesticity and tending to her chieftain husband's home. Once married, she began her first foray into piracy on the Irish Sea, convincing some of her husband's men to join her in attacking merchant ships headed for nearby Galway. But when her husband died in battle, she returned to her father's land to launch her career as a pirate in earnest. The legend of the Pirate Queen of Ireland was born.

Sifting myth from folklore, tradition and historical fact is not easy. Though not so well known outside her native land, Grace is lionized as an icon of Irish womanhood and commemorated on the sides of Irish ships, in folk songs and in James Joyce's *Finnegans Wake*. Even today, Howth Castle in County Dublin lays an extra place at dinner for an unexpected visitor – thanks to Grace.

After finding the family had locked its gates against her, she abducted their young heir as revenge, only returning him after she had extracted an eternal promise of hospitality.

For decades, her galleys would terrify traders and frustrate competing Irish clans as well as the English authorities. If any ship dared to reject her levies for safe passage in Clew Bay, where Grace's crew sailed from her well-established strongholds, they would be ruthlessly plundered.

Grace led by example. Oral tradition holds that she gave birth on one of her ships. In Catholic custom, women had to be blessed after childbirth before they were allowed to re-enter church; Grace, far from land, was a long way from the nearest priest. But when her ship came under attack by Algerian pirates, neither religious faith nor post-childbirth fatigue could stop her from joining in. Leaving her newborn son below deck, she rallied her troops, firing a musket at her enemy with the declaration, "Take this from unconsecrated hands!"[5]

But even as Grace terrorized the seas, England's grip on Ireland was tightening. The disparate and disunited Irish clans would never effectively band together to fight off their English conquerors. When Sir Richard Bingham was appointed by the crown as the new governor of Connaught, he launched a campaign of aggression against Grace and every other chieftain in the land, declaring, "The Irish were never tamed with words but with swords."[6] By the time Grace hit her sixties, the Dorset-born military man had subdued and decimated the Irish clans; seized her ships, cattle and horses, and had her eldest son murdered. With Bingham's warships docked in her beloved Clew Bay, she was effectively landlocked.

But Grace had a cunning ability to outmanoeuvre her enemies, even as they had her against the wall. She petitioned Queen Elizabeth I, pleading unjust impoverishment and offering to surrender some of her family's territory if the queen granted her the freedom to take to the seas again. It was a ruse, of course, to go above Bingham's head and seek favour with a higher power.

Writing letters to the queen was risky enough, but when Bingham captured one of Grace's remaining sons and sentenced him to hang for treason, Grace shocked everyone by heading straight to London to negotiate with Elizabeth I directly.

Good Queen Bess met the Pirate Queen in person, and while no records exist of their conversation, Grace must have left triumphant – for the queen herself ordered the release of Grace's son and granted permission for her to ply her trade on the seas again. And even as other Irish chiefs continued to fight a losing battle against their English oppressors, Grace's political nous resulted in her family thriving long into the next century. One of the last recorded mentions of the Pirate Queen was written by an English captain, who fought off one of her ships – even as an old woman, it seems, Grace never lost her taste for the sea.

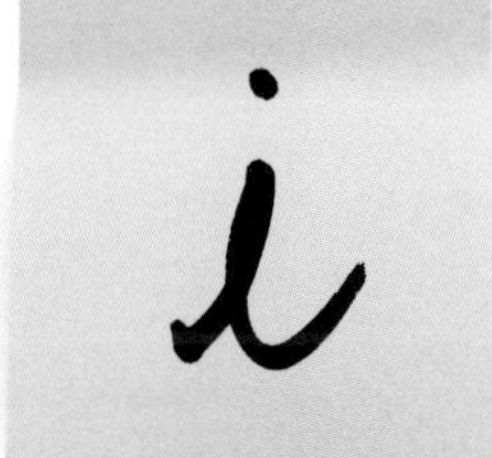

n an age when most European queens could rule only as the wife of a monarch, **Christina of Sweden** (1626–1689) sat on the Swedish throne as a king. And she confounded the expectations of almost everyone she encountered: at a time when women were expected to be prim and retiring, Christina wore men's clothing and rode horses side-saddle with guns at her hip. Most scandalously of all, she wound up abdicating her throne in order to gallivant across Europe, and she cultivated passionate friendships – and apparent love affairs – with men and women. Her behaviour was considered so unfeminine that an anthropologist exhumed her remains in 1965 to check if she was intersex (the results were inconclusive).

"I was born covered with hair; my voice was strong and harsh," she wrote in her memoirs.[7] Even Christina's birth confounded those around her; she was born with a caul wrapped around her, and her loud screams convinced nurses that she was a hoped-for royal male. King Gustav II Adolf, Christina's father, took the apparent disappointment in his stride. "She will undoubtedly be a clever woman," he declared, "for even at her birth she has succeeded in deceiving us all."[8]

His words would prove prophetic; Christina could speak three languages at the age of 12 and was reading Thucydides in Greek by the time she was a teenager. But her demeanour worried her mother: as a child, Christina would stride manfully around the palace, deploying swearwords that she had picked up from the stableboys.

When her father was killed in battle in 1632, Christina ascended the throne at the age of six but was not crowned king till she turned 18. Her childhood hero – other than her beloved father – was Alexander the Great, and she took to politics with the

seriousness it required. Her tomboyish habits matured into a casual disregard for courtly fashion. Her ladies-in-waiting were astonished by her tendency to wash and get dressed in 15 minutes flat, often grabbing whatever garment was nearest.

As king, Christina was frustrated with her uncultured court, which was more preoccupied with drinking than with books and learning. Described as the "Sibyl of the North", Christina was a voracious reader at a time when Sweden was considered an undeveloped backwater, and she invited scholars from across Europe to visit her kingdom. But her love of knowledge didn't always work out well for the thinkers she enticed to the cold shores of Sweden – the philosopher René Descartes famously perished of pneumonia in her kingdom.

Despite her intellect, Christina did not take well to the pressures of ruling. She rose early and went to bed late to keep up with all the duties her job demanded, but felt assailed by the never-ending stream of ministers and political secretaries. "State affairs take up all my time and weary me to death,"[9] she wrote in a letter to a French diplomat. She began to hatch a plan: What would happen if she abdicated the throne?

Abdication was by no means a simple matter; Christina knew it could plunge Sweden into civil war. But she felt hemmed in on all sides, not least because she was also coming under pressure to marry and produce an heir. According to Christina, however, she "felt such a repulsion towards the marital state that she would rather choose death than a man".[10] Her close friendship with the noblewoman Ebba Sparre could have contributed to her aversion to marriage. Christina once introduced Ebba as her "bedfellow" and wrote passionate letters to the lady-in-waiting: "I belong to you so utterly, that it will never be possible for you to lose me; and only when I die, shall I cease loving you."[11]

In February 1654, Christina finally announced her decision to abdicate in favour of her cousin, Charles Gustav, and within three days of her abdication in June, she was galloping out of Stockholm disguised as a man and headed for Rome. She quickly became a cause célèbre in Europe; nobody could understand why she had given up a royal title to become a commoner. Christina caused scandal everywhere she went, not least because of her unconventional dress and her great intelligence. "She is determined to appear like an Amazon," one French duke recounted. "She is as wild and as proud as her father, the Great Gustav…She knows more than our Academy and the Sorbonne put together."[12] She managed to scandalize her Lutheran homeland even further by converting to Catholicism, becoming Rome's most famous convert. And if anyone tried to rebuke her, she simply reminded them that she had given up all the riches in the world to do what she wished – and nobody could disagree with that.

But a commoner's life did not suit Christina. She struggled with her finances, and she launched half-baked schemes to re-enter politics, including a vague plan to become king of Naples (it never happened). She was always the subject of gossip – Europe was awash with rumours of her liaisons with both sexes – and this chattering sometimes exploded into full-on enmity, not least when Christina unknowingly violated some genteel social norm or other.

In her later years, Christina corresponded with politicians and diplomats all over Europe and became a sharp observer of current affairs. She died of a fever at the age of 62 – a monarch who had given up everything to pursue adventures of her own and never showed a trace of regret over it. As she confided to Ebba in a letter, "I am beginning to think that Majesty lends neither virtues nor enlightenment and that one can be a very powerful king and, at the same time, a very insignificant human being both in good fortune and in adversity."[13]

hen **Doria Shafik** (1908–1975) was sentenced to house arrest at the age of 48, poetry and literature became her escape. She spent the next 18 years sequestered in her sixth-floor apartment in Cairo. Egypt's pioneering activist faded from public memory until her 1975 suicide reignited her status as the country's most ambitious – and tragically thwarted – women's rights campaigner.

Doria was born into a middle-class Egyptian family in 1908, at a time of unique transition. Women were still expected to marry after receiving minimal schooling, but Doria had the luck – and the will – to fight for her education. At 19, she sailed from Alexandria to France, where she dived into her studies at the Sorbonne. Europe was both a revelation and a shock. At the International House in Paris, a sort of dormitory for women students, she met women from many other countries – from Martinique to Morocco and Greece – and began to refine her understanding of the torment and prejudice experienced by her gender.

"I realized that my country was not the only place where women suffered," she wrote of her time there. "We each had the experience of being misunderstood in our own countries, being intellectually more ambitious than our countrymen."[14]

Completing the *Licence libre* and the *Licence d'état* was not easy – the two were separate degrees, and one required Doria to quickly learn Latin, a language of which she previously had no knowledge. Still, Doria pulled it off. A few years later, she would successfully defend her doctorate with a thesis that argued the link between women's rights and Islam.

But Doria was no bookish recluse; while back home for the holidays, she competed in the Miss Universe heats in Alexandria ("I wanted to amuse myself a little," she told a French reporter with a smile). She was the first Egyptian Muslim woman to enter the competition and came second to a contestant who would later go on to become Miss Universe.

The Egyptian press, which had previously celebrated her as a national figure of educational achievement, turned nasty and accused her of acting in an un-Islamic fashion. But Doria saw no contradiction between participating in a beauty contest and her religious or political beliefs. "In Paris," she said, "I had asserted myself in the intellectual sphere. Now I wanted to assert myself in the feminine sphere."[15]

When Doria, armed with her doctorate, finally returned to Egypt for good, her application for a teaching job at the University of Cairo was rejected (the damning assessment: "too modern"[16]). But Egypt had changed while Doria was in Paris – now political upheaval was in the air. Though Britain had granted independence to its former protectorate in 1922, there was simmering discontent with the lingering presence of British imperialism. Doria firmly believed that women had a key part to play in Egypt's struggle for liberation and that feminism would help both genders get there. "Feminism," she wrote in an essay in 1944, "in the true sense of the word is the total comprehension between man and woman, not a perpetual fight between the two sexes."[17]

When she was offered a job as the editor-in-chief of *La Femme Nouvelle*, a French-language magazine associated with Princess Chevikar, the powerful wife of King Fuad, she leaped at the chance to explore these ideas on a larger literary platform. But it would also place her in direct opposition to mainstream political sentiment, which saw the monarchy as an out-of-touch relic on the side of the British. Undeterred, Doria's solution to satisfying her critics was to start a more political magazine, this time in Arabic: *Bint al-Nil* ("Daughter of the Nile").

As Egyptian society splintered between the Muslim Brotherhood, the Communists and the military, Doria became convinced that the country needed to pass legislation that would allow women to vote and run for office. "Women must not only be present when laws concerning them are legislated; they must be involved in writing them," she argued. "By demanding the totality of her rights, particularly her political rights, which are the very basis of all rights, the woman could bring about fundamental changes in society."[18]

She founded the Bint al-Nil Union, announcing it as a new movement that would bring about emancipation for all Egyptian women. In February 1951, she led a group of almost 1,500 women to the gates of the Egyptian parliament to issue a series of demands, including universal suffrage. Over the next few months, Egyptians took to the streets to rage against the monarchy and the government, leading to riots and the 1952 military coup that overthrew the regime. Doria was ecstatic at the hope of change and turned Bint al-Nil into a political party. Women, she thought, would finally carve out their place in the newly declared Egyptian republic.

The next few years were a bitter disappointment. As the military junta cracked down on dissent, the all-male ruling party began to draw up a new constitution without promising any political rights to women. With a group of eight women, Doria went on hunger strike in protest. The reaction was explosive; Doria and her group were hailed as 20th-century suffragettes in the international media. Eight days into the hunger strike, and under the glare of the world's press, the new government relented: women would be allowed full constitutional rights in the new Egypt.

Post-hunger strike, Doria was an international celebrity and embarked on a lecture tour around the world. But back in Egypt, President Gamal Abdel Nasser was consolidating his authority and weeding out opposition – and Doria, with her newfound links to the West, was an object of suspicion. On her return, Doria staged a second hunger strike to protest the encroaching dictatorship of her country.

It was to be her final, lone act of public protest. She was widely denounced in Egypt, and even her old supporters were terrified of speaking out. Nasser gave women the right to vote, but Doria did not reap the benefits of women's entry into public life – in 1957, Nasser condemned her to house arrest and blacklisted her name in the press. Her own political party expelled her, and she was branded a traitor to the revolution.

Even after the government informally lifted her house arrest, she remained indoors – the betrayal of her allies and her countrymen had stung too much. She spent almost 20 years in near-total isolation, with only visits from family to break her solitude. She was 66 when she tumbled from the balcony of her apartment, her death reawakening public consciousness of this once ubiquitous public figure and making her warning against tyranny all the more resonant.

Over her decades in public life, Doria had never yielded and never backed down – it was her own country that failed her. She stayed true to the words she had written when she was 19: "To Want and To Dare! Never hesitate to act when the feeling of injustice revolts us."[19]

hen **Lakshmibai** (*c.* 1828–1858) was born in the sacred Hindu city of Varanasi around 1828, the British East India Company had rapidly expanded across India and were effectively the rulers of much of the land. But the country's long-held resentment and disquiet would finally erupt with the Indian Rebellion – and Lakshmibai would prove to be one of its greatest heroines.

She was only 14 when she married Gangadhar Rao, the Maharaja of Jhansi, a princely and rich state in what is now Uttar Pradesh. But her husband died in 1853 without leaving a son. The traditional way to sidestep this misfortune was for the ruler to adopt a boy as the next in line to the throne, and he had done this on the day before he died. However, the British had other ideas. Under the so-called "doctrine of lapse", such adoptions took place at the discretion of the country's colonial rulers, and the Governor-General of India refused to acknowledge Gangadhar's chosen heir. The state of Jhansi – previously ruled by its own line of monarchs – was promptly annexed.

Lakshmibai had grown into an intelligent and charismatic woman – and a lover of daily exercise. According to records, her daily regime would begin with wrestling and weightlifting at the crack of dawn, then horseback riding and the occasional elephant ride. One witness claimed that Lakshmibai rode horses with a sword in each hand and the reins gripped between her teeth. This physical fitness would serve her well in the years to come, though the 25-year-old queen first attempted to appeal against Britain's decision, declaring to one British lawyer, "I will not give up my Jhansi!"[20] repeatedly.

In 1857, rebellion began in the garrisons of Meerut, a city near Delhi, and spread south to the capital city Jhansi. Here, Hindu officers mutinied against their British superiors, plundering the city and slaughtering English men, women and children before leaving to join the rebel troops assembling in Agra and Delhi. Without the British in charge, Lakshmibai proclaimed herself the regent of Jhansi and began to prepare for war.

She held court with her prime minister every day, meting out justice in cases brought to her attention – sometimes dressed in men's clothes, with a sword hanging from a gold sash around her waist. "Dressed thus," one Brahmin priest in her court wrote, "she looked like an avatar of a warrior goddess."[21]

Her people adored their unusual queen, who could be found galloping around her fort at night in pitch darkness and carrying out enormous acts of charity. On one occasion, she summoned all the tailors in the town to stitch clothing so a thousand impoverished peasants could survive the winter. She was also said to have paid the bride price for a widowed Brahmin who was too poor to marry a second time, her only stipulation being, "When you do get married, you must send us an invitation."[22]

Even as Lakshmibai blossomed into a kind and just ruler, the British were assembling their forces with the intention of suppressing every last trace of independence in the region by any means necessary. Historians now debate how much involvement Lakshmibai had in the massacre of British troops at Jhansi, but some contemporary reports were in no doubt as to her complicity with the mutineers. "The Jezebel of India was there," wrote one British army doctor of Lakshmibai in her city, "the young, energetic, proud, unbending, uncompromising Ranee, and upon her head rested the blood of the slain, and a punishment as awful awaited her."[23]

Lakshmibai had prepared for the British to lay siege to her city, and she rode into battle – but her city's defences were no match for the hailstorm of cannonballs that battered its walls. She refused to surrender, even after enemy soldiers forced their way into Jhansi, looting her beloved subjects' homes and executing every man over the age of 16. Lakshmibai retreated from the city and launched a successful attack with other rebels on Gwalior, a strategically placed fort city some 100km (60 miles) away. It would be her last stand.

"This Indian Joan of Arc was dressed in a red jacket and trousers and a white turban," wrote Sir Owen Burne, then a military secretary to the British commander of the attack. She only conceded defeat in death and, even then, spent her last moments giving back to the people she had fought so hard for. "She wore Scindia's celebrated pearl necklace. As she lay mortally wounded in her tent, she ordered these ornaments to be distributed among her troops."[24] The rebellion had ended in failure, but something of her spirit lingered to see India overthrow the British Raj in the 20th century – with the Indian National Army naming its women's regiment after her.

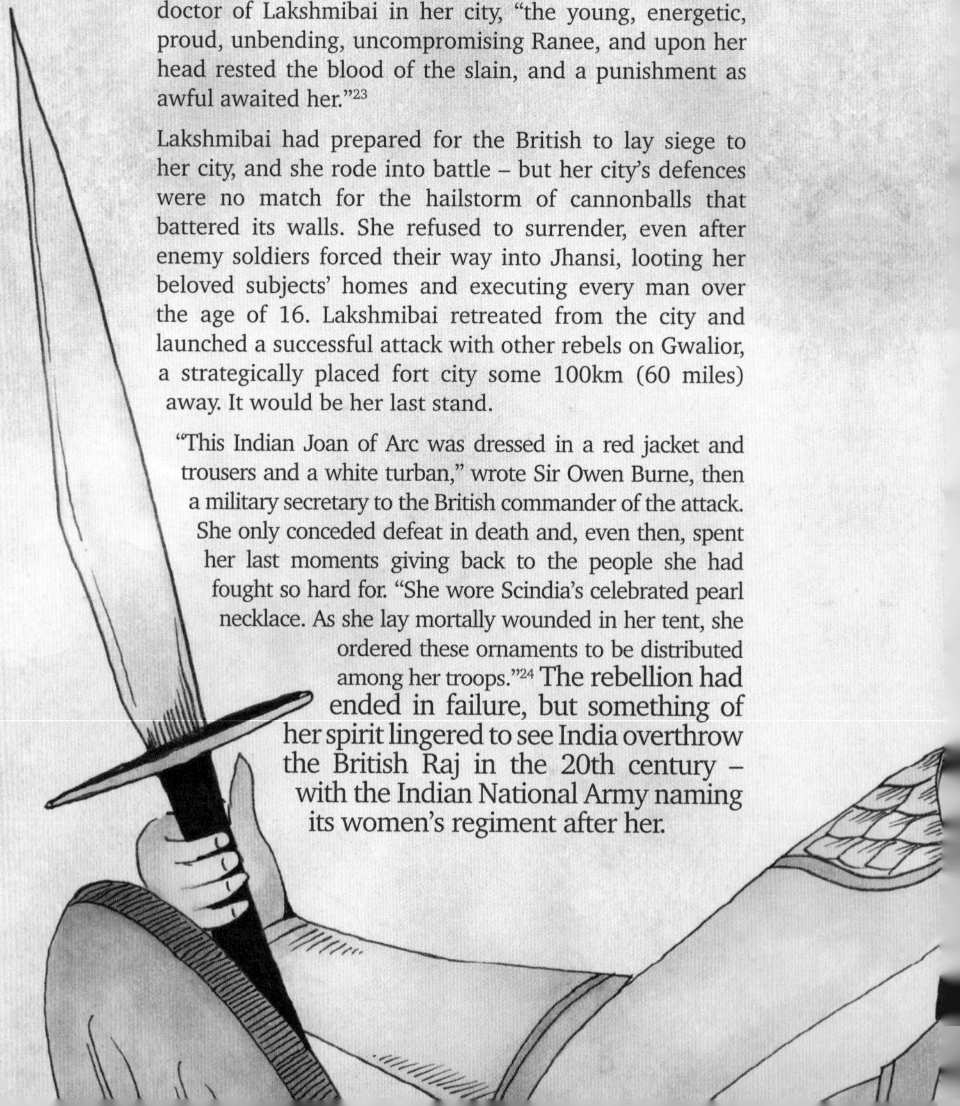

merica's long history of espionage didn't start with the CIA. Even before it wrested independence from Britain, the country was fertile ground for spooks and secret agents. Founding father George Washington wasn't just a brilliant military general – he was also the country's first spymaster, and a hugely astute one at that. His spy network, the Culper Ring, operated around British-occupied New York, funnelling secrets and information that would help to lead the Americans to victory.

Women were a vital part of the American Revolution. As camp followers to Washington's army, they served as cooks, nurses and washerwomen. But some women were also engaged in more cloak-and-dagger activities – and none more so than **Agent 355** (dates unknown).

In New York, women were uniquely placed to spy on the British. As society hostesses or servants, they had direct contact with members of the ruling elite and yet passed completely unnoticed. Because of their gender, they barely qualified completely as a threat in the eyes of the British – and Washington's spy ring exploited that presumption to the fullest.

Described as "the hidden daughter of the American Revolution,"[25] Agent 355 is widely believed to have been one of the first female spooks in US history – and because she went to the grave with her secrets and identity concealed, she is probably one of the most successful.

Agent 355 is thought to have been a young socialite, described by leading Culper Ring member Abraham Woodhull as a "[lady] of my acquaintance" who was well suited to "out wit them all".[26] He took care not to record her name – the label "355" was derived from the Culper Ring code, which used numbers to disguise secret messages and identities. For instance, 237 referred to "gentleman"; according to the code, 355 meant "lady".

Her biggest coup? Helping to uncover Benedict Arnold's treachery when the turncoat general switched sides and plotted against his own countrymen. She also helped to take down Major John André, the British Army intelligence officer in cahoots with Arnold to hand over a key fort in West Point, New York, to Britain. The details of Arnold's deal were gleaned from information that Agent 355 had extracted on one of the many nights that she spent socializing and charming drunken British soldiers, André included. He was later captured en route to West Point and executed as a spy.

André's death and the discovery of Arnold's plot also spelled disaster for 355. In a letter to a Culper Ring member on 12 November, Woodhull revealed that an "ever serviceable"[27] friend had been captured by the enemy. It is widely believed that the "friend" was Agent 355, who was condemned to the HMS *Jersey*, a prison ship moored near Brooklyn. These floating jails were called "death ships" for good reason: prisoners were crammed below deck in festering conditions, with only vermin and the fetid corpses of their fellow ex-inmates for company. HMS *Jersey* was the worst of the lot – its nickname was "Hell". Some eight thousand people in New York were left to perish in these death ships, and it is likely that Agent 355 met her end there.

To this day, historians are divided on the identity of Agent 355. Some argue that Anna Smith Strong, the daughter of a judge, had an incentive to rebel against the British, as they had thrown her husband into jail. Another theory holds that Elizabeth Burgin, a widow who secretly helped American prisoners escape from British prison ships, had the know-how necessary for subterfuge. Some historians scoff that 355 may not even have existed as a single individual – it may have been used as a collective code name by a number of different women.

More than two hundred years later, we are none the wiser as to 355's true identity, or her motivations for joining such a perilous, and ultimately fatal, spy mission. The history of the United States is full of patriots in petticoats, but Agent 355 is perhaps the most mysterious of them all.

xecuted with a bullet at Dachau concentration camp, **Noor Inayat Khan** (1914–1944) died with the word *liberté* on her lips. It was September 1944 – eight long months before Germany would surrender to the Allies – and the 30-year-old had been captured as a spy for the French Resistance. The Nazis had classed her as one of their most dangerous prisoners, marked for death as part of Hitler's *Nacht und Nebel* directive – and like the "night and fog", after which the directive was named, the intention was for her to disappear without a trace. By the time the bullet took her life, she had already been shackled in solitary confinement for ten months.

Noor was not just one of Germany's greatest enemies; she was also a Muslim, an avowed pacifist, a children's author who penned gentle folk tales, the daughter of a Sufi preacher and a descendant of Tipu Sultan, the 18th-century leader of the Indian kingdom of Mysore. In addition, she was a passionate supporter of India's freedom from colonial rule, telling her 1942 interview panel at the Women's Auxiliary Air Force (WAAF) that she might well end up fighting them on the other side of the battleground for Indian independence – as soon as the simple matter of World War II was wrapped up, of course.

Born on 1 January 1914, Noor spent her early years in London before her family sailed across the English Channel to settle on the outskirts of Paris, where she perfected her French. She began to carve out a life for herself as a writer for *Le Figaro*, eventually publishing a book of children's stories entitled *Twenty Jataka Tales* in 1939. Then, in 1940, German forces invaded France. Noor's parents had raised their children to believe in non-violence, and although Noor herself had no love for the British, the Nazis posed a threat that she could not reconcile with her values. As her biographer Shrabani Basu explains, Noor and her brother

Vilayet resolved to do what they could to help; when their family fled to the safety of London, they both signed up in their old hometown to fight the scourge of fascism.

While Vilayet volunteered with the Royal Air Force, Noor passed her interview at the WAAF and began training as a radio operator, transmitting messages to those involved in the war effort. Then espionage came knocking in the form of the Special Operations Executive, Britain's wartime spy organization. Lured by the promise of recruiting a spy who spoke fluent French and knew the lie of the land in Paris, they reached out to Noor with an offer: would she join them as an agent? She would be sent back to her beloved France as an undercover operative, with no official protection and little support. There was no guarantee that she would not be killed if she was apprehended. She accepted.

By the time Noor was smuggled into enemy-occupied territory, the French Resistance was beginning to fall apart. Within a few weeks, the Gestapo had arrested most of her comrades, and the few who remained had fled to the safety of Britain. Noor was asked to return home, but she refused to abandon her post. She became the de facto leader of the spy cell – the sole link between the underground Resistance and England – and quickly set about the dangerous task of rebuilding the network. For several months, she transmitted intercepted messages back to the British while evading capture. One of the only things the Nazis had to go on was her code name: Madeleine.

But Noor's luck ran out when someone sold her out to the Gestapo for the bounty of 100,000 francs. While in custody she attempted escape twice: once, immediately after she was captured, and a second time with two other prisoners, dislodging the bars on their window and climbing out on to the roof – only to be discovered when an RAF bombing mission set off the air-raid sirens, prompting the guards to check their room.

The Germans did not take kindly to her escape attempts. At Pforzheim prison, she was repeatedly beaten and tortured for the better part of a year in solitary confinement, but she still refused to give up any information to her captors. Finally, she was sent to Dachau, where she was executed. In 1949, her bravery was posthumously rewarded by Britain with the George Cross, and by France with the Croix de Guerre. In 2012, Princess Anne unveiled a bronze statue in her memory in Bloomsbury, London, a short distance away from her old home in the city.

One ceremony attendee, a 91-year-old woman who had met Noor on a Morse code training course, told a reporter from the *Camden New Journal* how, after the war, "there were banner headlines, 'So-and-so awarded George Cross'. I couldn't believe it was Noor, but she deserved it, oh yes."

hen Queen **Njinga Mbandi** (1581/2–1663), also known as Nzinga Mbande, was born, the Portuguese empire was busy wrapping its tentacles around Africa. The slave trade was booming, and the unquenchable demand for labour in the New World drove Portugal to seek control of southwest Africa. Against this backdrop, Njinga spent her life battling the occupiers of her land, skilfully playing her rivals off against each other to preserve the existence of her kingdom.

Njinga seemed almost ordained from birth to fulfil the role: she was born in the breech position, with the umbilical cord coiled around her neck. According to local superstition, this signalled that the child was destined to live a singular life. Though she was the child of a concubine, her father, the king of the Mbundu people, favoured his bright and brilliant daughter, allowing her to accompany him on royal business – a privilege usually afforded to the sons of kings.

Despite these pleasures, Njinga grew up knowing that her father's kingdom was on the run. Only a year after her birth, her family and their court had been forced to abandon their capital in the face of a Portuguese attack. Her great-grandfather's kingdom of Ndongo was seized and renamed Angola, with the port city of Luanda as its new base. Portuguese and indigenous slave raiders also ravaged the Mbundu people, tearing families apart to work on plantations or transporting them to foreign colonies.

When Njinga's father died, her brother Ngola inherited the throne. He immediately set about eliminating potential rivals – a merciless campaign of bloodshed that included murdering Njinga's own son. He even had Njinga and her sisters sterilized by pouring boiling oil on their bellies. For all his bloodthirstiness however, Ngola could not beat back the Portuguese forces sweeping through his kingdom. Over the course of just four years, more than 55,000 Mbundus were abducted and sold into slavery.

There was no other option but peace. In 1622, Njinga travelled to Luanda to negotiate with Correia de Sousa, the new Portuguese governor of Angola. However, she was aghast when de Sousa did not offer her a chair while receiving her – a sure sign that the negotiations were off to an unequal start. She quickly ordered a servant to get down on all fours and offer up their back as a substitute seat.[28] This bold reassertion of status impressed one onlooker so much that he later turned it into an illustration, which is one of the few eyewitness depictions of the African queen. In order to seal the peace deal, Njinga even converted to Catholicism in Luanda and was christened Dona Ana de Sousa.

But when Correia de Sousa was replaced by a new Portuguese governor, the unsteady peace between Ndongo and Portugal collapsed. Her brother died unexpectedly – some say as a result of poison administered by Njinga – and she seized the throne and declared herself queen. Njinga's claim to power was disputed by both Portugal and internal factions within Ndongo, as the kingdom had never been ruled by a woman. The Portuguese installed a puppet ruler in Ndongo and attempted to drive Njinga out of her own kingdom.

From then on, her attitude toward the Portuguese became decidedly more aggressive. In order to expand her army, she recruited help from the Imbangala, a fearsome band of mercenaries and warriors. She also offered refuge to runaway slaves from Portuguese plantations to boost her manpower.

By 1629, however, she was out of options – the Portuguese had driven her from Ndongo, and her Imbangala allies had betrayed her. Instead, she cast her gaze northeast to Matamba, a kingdom with a conveniently historic lineage of female queens. She quickly moved her capital there, and from that vantage point proved to be a constant thorn in the Portuguese side, launching attacks on their trade routes and diverting slaves – and therefore wealth – into Matamba.

Long into her sixties, Njinga dogged her enemy at every turn. Dressed as a man, she rode out into battle with her troops, and even trained her own ladies-in-waiting to become her personal battalion. Even more unusually, she took several men as lovers and made them her concubines, ordering them to dress in women's clothes and sleep in the same quarters as her female servants. (The men were executed if they dared to touch her maids.)

She was 74 by the time she entered into a peace treaty with the Portuguese. Her old allies, the Dutch, had been expelled from Luanda, and Njinga had been worn down by decades of war. She would die one of Africa's most successful leaders – among its kings and queens alike – in repelling colonial forces.

irginia Hall (1906–1982) was a woman of many identities: Marie Monin, Germaine, Marie of Lyon and Camille, to name just a few. But the one that stuck was a nickname created by her sworn enemies in the Gestapo: the Limping Lady. There was good reason for that moniker, though Virginia personally found it rather offensive – the "most dangerous of all Allied spies", [29] as the Gestapo also called her, walked with a wooden leg. The leg even had its own nickname: Cuthbert.

As the US waded through the worst of the Great Depression, Virginia escaped her native Baltimore for Turkey, where she found work as a clerk at the American Consulate in Smyrna, the ancient Greek city now known as Izmir. Her greatest ambition was to work for the Foreign Service, but a freak hunting accident demolished her hopes when her shotgun accidentally went off and blasted her foot to smithereens. Doctors determined that the only way to save her was to amputate her leg below the knee – and, unfortunately, the Foreign Service had no use for a disabled female diplomat with a prosthetic limb. As the letter that spelled the demise of her dream put it, the amputation of any limb was cause for immediate rejection.

But rejection and her self-described "bitter disappointment" didn't stop her from joining the Ambulance Corps in France as World War II broke out across Europe. And when a chance encounter on a train with an officer of the Special Operations Executive (SOE) led to her recruitment for this clandestine paramilitary group, which had been set up under Winston Churchill's instructions to "set Europe ablaze", so much the better. This was the ultimate diplomatic assignment – and she didn't even need to be part of the Foreign Service to take it on.

Adopting a false identity as a *New York Post* reporter assigned to cover Vichy France, Virginia was the first female SOE agent in France. She organized the nascent spy network and helped to spirit away prisoners of war, all the while knowing that her capture would mean torture and certain death. She kept her nerve until November 1942, when Germany took control of Vichy France, forcing her to flee over the snow-tipped Pyrenees mountain range. When she told her handlers that her leg was slowing her down, she received the cryptic reply, "If Cuthbert tiresome, have him eliminated."[30] Fortunately, she did make it to safety.

However, this wasn't the last that Nazi-occupied France saw of Virginia. Displaying the same tenacity that drove her to the SOE, she signed up with the US Office of Strategic Services (OSS) – the wartime precursor to the CIA – and returned to France by way of a torpedo boat. She was tasked with transmitting information back to the Allies about German troop movements and scouting potential locations for parachute drops of supplies and arms.

Disguised as an old peasant woman, Virginia smothered her frame in bulky layers of sweaters and matronly skirts, perfecting a doddery shuffle that helped to disguise her limp. She even changed all her dental fillings to look like those used by French dentists. Once behind enemy lines in Haute-Loire, Virginia met with a French farmer loosely allied with the Resistance; he supplied her with a herd of livestock that she moved from pasture to pasture – the perfect cover for someone who needed to stay on the move and keep a lookout for discreet drop zones.

But her assignment in the French countryside was far from bucolic. The Germans knew that the Resistance was

organizing against them and were not averse to shooting civilians suspected of subterfuge. Four townspeople were executed, their bodies mounted on spikes and left to rot in public. Virginia sent a message to London: "WOLVES AT THE DOOR. STOP."

Still Virginia wasn't fazed: in the run-up to D-Day, she trained three battalions of Resistance freedom fighters to wage combat against Germany. On her instructions, they destroyed roads, blew up bridges and derailed trains – anything that would sabotage the German war machine. One band of guerrillas trapped a Nazi convoy and killed 150 soldiers, capturing another 500. At its largest, the de facto army she directed comprised almost 1,500 men.

When the war ended, the White House announced President Harry S. Truman's intention to award Virginia the Distinguished Service Cross for her "extraordinary heroism". But Virginia shied away from public accolades – she hadn't even publicized the honorary MBE (Member of the Order of the British Empire) she received from King George VI in 1943 – and wasn't quite ready to give up her work. "[She] feels very strongly that she should not receive any publicity or any announcement," a cable from the Paris OSS read. "She states that she is still operational and most anxious to get busy."[31] And she did: as the OSS evolved into the present-day CIA, she became one of its first female agents. As ever, Virginia was one step ahead of everyone else.

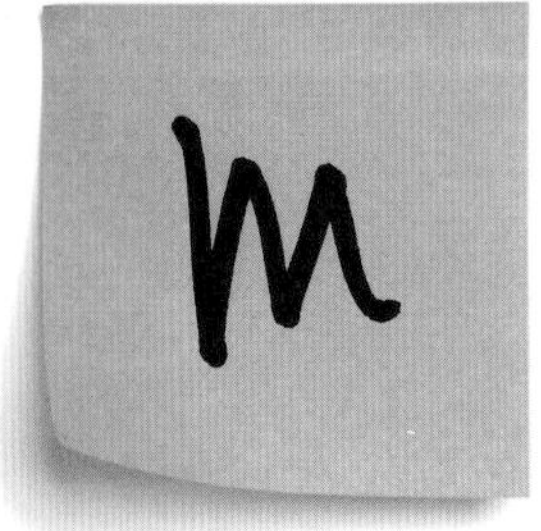

adagascar, an island off the coast of southeast Africa, is a difficult place to conquer. In size about halfway between Texas and California, or twice the size of the UK, it includes mountainous central highlands, swampy rainforests and desert savannah. The largest ethnic group of Madagascar's Malagasy people is the Merina of the central highlands. For more than three centuries, the kings and queens of the Merina kingdom sought to unify the distant lands and repel outside forces – and none more so than Queen **Ranavalona I** (1778–1861), the so-called "Mad Queen of Madagascar".

Ranavalona inherited the throne under inauspicious circumstances, following the death of her husband King Radama I. Despite having been the first of the king's 12 wives, her claim to power was tenuous, and she had to move quickly to consolidate power after her coronation. The result was a 33-year reign, marked by shrewd political manoeuvring and ruthlessness, culminating in bloodshed that saw her labelled the "Female Caligula".

Nineteenth-century Malagasy society was a harsh and unforgiving place. As the first Merina queen, Ranavalona's immediate act was to execute her rivals and their families, as Radama had done before her. She inherited a system of forced labour, slavery and army conscription;[32] Radama had had a penchant for executing dissenters and letting dogs devour their corpses.[33] The kingdom was also poised at a tipping point, with European forces of colonization and evangelism creeping into the region.

Like Radama, Ranavalona saw the pragmatic benefits of allowing outsiders into the kingdom – the Europeans brought modernizing skills and crafts that Madagascar lacked, such as munition-making and arithmetic. During her reign, however, she was openly and aggressively hostile toward foreign forces seeking to operate in her homeland. (Given that Madagascar became a French colony after her demise, she may have been right to be suspicious.)

Radama had been the first to allow foreign missionaries to teach and proselytize in his kingdom, but the growing popularity of religion brought the missionaries and their new converts into conflict with Ranavalona and her court, which still practised traditional ancestor and idol worship. An increasing number of her subjects began openly to scorn and denounce these old beliefs, on one occasion driving the queen to tears. Still, she permitted the missionaries to continue to educate the population, even allowing them to reopen the schools six months before the end of the traditional mourning period for her husband.

But the turning point came when a powerful Malagasy chief came to Ranavalona, pleading for a spear with which to kill himself. He could not stand, he explained, to see the outsiders influence the country to dishonour their idols, the holy guardians of the nation, and neglect the ancestors who had protected the kingdom. Their supporters had already infiltrated every level of society, from the army to the government, and it would only be a matter of time until the missionaries told their governments that Madagascar was ripe for conquest. He concluded, "I do not wish to live to see that calamity come upon our country…therefore I ask a spear, to pierce my heart, that I may die before that evil day comes."[34]

Ranavalona wept with rage and swore revenge on all Christians. In a royal edict, she commanded that none of her Malagasy subjects was to take part in any Christian services. Any converts were given one month – later amended to a week – to hand themselves in and recant their beliefs, on penalty of death. Fearing for their lives, most Malagasy Christians gave themselves up and were punished with fines. Those in the armed forces or government were stripped of their rank and income. The queen did not order the missionaries out of the country, allowing them to continue teaching non-religious subjects, though the majority left for more tolerant lands by the middle of the year.

But Christianity had put down its roots in Madagascar. Even after the last missionaries departed, a group of Malagasy Christians continued to covertly practise their faith and were subject to enormous persecution. Thousands were punished, jailed, forced into slavery or killed. One traveller to Madagascar lamented, "Blood – and always blood – is the maxim of Queen Ranavalona, and every day seems lost to this wicked woman on which she cannot sign at least half a dozen death-warrants."[35]

The same went for Ranavalona's opponents, or anyone who stood in the way of her military campaign to control the whole island. The tradition of forced labour conscripted thousands into her army, many of whom perished in her quest to bring the whole of Madagascar and its numerous principalities to heel. Her pitiless reign is even thought to have sliced the population of the island from five million to half that number between 1833 and 1839.

All of Ranavalona's attempts to resist foreign conquest – by any means necessary – came to nought. She was succeeded by her more liberal son, who converted to Christianity, restored relations with Europe and refused to perform many of the ceremonies that Ranavalona had fought so hard to preserve.[36] Today, many Malagasy regard her as a tyrannical queen, and her name is even used as a derogatory insult for a controlling, overbearing woman.[37]

But Ranavalona may have had some semblance of revenge. As her reformist son recanted the beliefs and practices of his traditionalist mother, spirit possession took hold of the land. En masse, Malagasy people would dance hysterically in public mobs until exhaustion gripped them. It was, they said, the spirit of Ranavalona taking hold of their bodies, forcing them to return to the old rituals.

hen Europeans colonized Australia, they did not land on a barren, uninhabited continent. They were met by Aboriginal people, who had already been there for roughly 55,000 years. But the settlers brought mayhem, death and violence – driving one Aboriginal woman to inflict it on them in return.

Tarenorerer (1800–1831), also known as Walyer, was born near Emu Bay on the northwestern coast of the island of Tasmania (then known as Van Diemen's Land), to a tribe that spoke the Tommeginne language. As a teenager, she was kidnapped by another tribe and sold off to white men living on the Bass Strait Islands, a chain of 50 islands in the strait that separates Tasmania from the Australian mainland.

This was not an unusual occurrence. Hunting and killing seals for their fur had become a lucrative trade; four species of seal had been recorded in the Bass Strait alone, and their skins were traded for tea and porcelain or sold as textiles. Aboriginal women from Tasmania were routinely abducted and forced into slavery at sealing camps, where they were raped, abused and forced to labour alongside settlers of the Bass Strait.

The Tasmanian frontier – almost 800km (500 miles) away from the administrative reach of Sydney – was a lawless and violent place. Those who washed up on its shores were convicts and outcasts from colonial society, and many saw no problem in trading – or treating – women as if they were cargo. Tarenorerer was renamed Walyer by her new masters, but years of subjugation did not break her will. By 1830, she had escaped and rejoined her community in northwest Tasmania, having learned the invaders' English tongue and gained knowledge of their firearms.

This information would prove useful when Tarenorerer came to lead a group of Aboriginal warriors – men, women and even children – intent on driving the settlers out of their land. She advised that they should strike the *luta tawin* (white men) in the moments after their guns discharged, just as they were scrambling to reload with more bullets. The guerrillas snuck into enemy camps to slaughter their livestock. One Aboriginal informant told G A Robinson, a prominent settler and conciliator between Aboriginal tribes and their European enemies, that Tarenorerer would fire her gun at huts in the camp, verbally abusing the sealers and daring them to come out and face her – whereupon they would be speared to death by her followers.

0 10 20 30 40 50
Kilometers

She reportedly said that she "liked a *luta tawin* as she did a black snake"[38] – which is to say, not very much at all. She became known as the "Amazon of Van Diemen's Land".

At the time, Robinson was engaged in a semi-altruistic quest to convince Tasmania's Aboriginal communities to lay down their arms and peaceably relocate to settlements on the islands of the Bass Strait. (He had also demanded £900 from the colonial government if he were to successfully remove all of them from the mainland, on top of a lifetime pension and his existing salary.) Tasmania was in the grip of the Black War, a frenzied guerrilla war that saw hundreds of European settlers killed at the hands of Aboriginal warriors. Two years before Tarenorerer's escape, politicians had declared martial law in Tasmania, effectively giving settlers legal impunity for murder. Robinson saw deportation as the more humane alternative to bloodshed.

By December of 1830, Tarenorerer had been captured and sold to a man hunting seals and muttonbirds on a tiny island in the Bass Strait. Robinson's men found her stewing away on the island, having failed to convince the other Aboriginal women on the desolate hunk of land to murder their captor and steal away in his boat. When she was finally hauled in to meet Robinson, she claimed to be called Mary Anne – but her identity was given away by her dog, Whiskey.

Robinson was overjoyed at the capture. Believing that Tarenorerer was responsible for "nearly all the mischief perpetrated upon the different settlements",[39] he kept her away from other Aboriginal people; he could not risk another Tarenorerer-led uprising. She was shipped out to an isolated island in the Bass Strait and died of influenza on 5 June 1831.

By 1832, almost all the Aboriginal people in Tasmania had been killed or forcibly removed to islands in the Bass Strait; many were tricked onto boats headed far away from their homes. There, like Tarenorerer, they died of disease. As for Robinson, he collected his reward – plus an additional 1,200 hectares (3,000 acres) of land – and expressed his hope that his extinction-causing campaign would inspire others. "Time is not far distant," he wrote, "when the same humane policy will be adopted towards the Aboriginal inhabitants of every colony throughout the British Empire."[40]

The Warriors

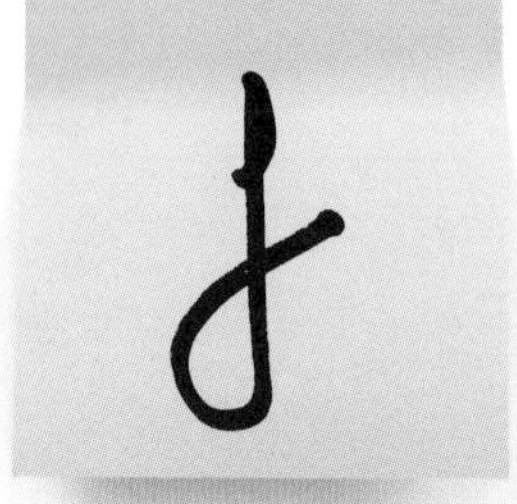

rom rebellion leaders to spirit goddesses and national martyrs, **The Trung sisters** (*c.* AD 12–43) have travelled through every label you can think of since their origins in the first century AD. Almost two thousand years later, Vietnam continues to celebrate the anniversary of their uprising on the sixth day of the lunar month, when incense is lit for the two long-departed women.

Trung Trac and Trung Nhi – Trac being the elder – were born into an aristocratic, landowning family in Giao Chi, a northern province of Vietnam, under Han Dynasty rule. For more than a century, the Chinese had governed its neighbour to the south, but the Vietnamese were growing increasingly unhappy with their harsh subjugation under foreign laws and customs, which governed everything from agriculture to land rights. China, for instance, observed an inheritance system, in which land was passed down through fathers and sons – an unthinkable custom to the Vietnamese, who believed that property should be passed down from mother to daughter.[1]

Some sources claim that Trac's nobleman husband, Thi Sach, spoke out against these reforms and was killed on the orders of the Han governor, driving Trac and her sister to take up arms against the Chinese. Others hold that it was simply the love of their people and a sense of burning injustice that led the siblings to instigate the country's first-ever uprising against China. Either way, the pair armed themselves in AD 40 and led their troops into war, drawing 80,000 people to their cause and clawing back 65 cities from the Chinese. That two women could have led their country in an armed insurgency may seem remarkable, but the Trung sisters were not the only women fighting for independence. It is said that one noblewoman, Phung Thi Chinh, was heavily pregnant when she joined the rebel army – pausing on the battlefield only to give birth before fighting her way out of the scrum.[2]

Once the sisters' troops had successfully forced China out of northern Vietnam, Trung Trac was declared queen[3] and set up her royal court in Mê Linh with Nhi by her side. But the Han rulers were not about to roll over without a fight; instead, they sent their most fearsome general, Ma Yuan, and his army to brutally suppress the rebellion. The Chinese reconquered Vietnam and crushed the Trung sisters' rebel forces. It is said that the pair were then caught and beheaded by Ma Yuan, though other sources say that they both leaped into the river and drowned, preferring suicide to capture. (According to one legend, the sisters' bodies floated down the river and were transformed into two stone sentinels, which still radiate light to scare off any enemy boats.[4])

The Trung sisters' rebellion lasted only two years, but their exploits soon became legendary. They were remembered in epic song and poetry, and, as the centuries passed, the siblings were transformed into objects of worship.

According to 12th-century records, a Vietnamese king visited their ancestral temple to pray for rain. When the heavens opened, he fell asleep and had a vision of two women wearing crowns, on the backs of steel horses. "We are the two Trung sisters," they declared. "By the order of God on high, we have made rain."[5] He built two temples in their name and declared the sisters "Chaste Divine Ladies" by imperial appointment – a tradition of honour followed by subsequent kings in the 13th and 14th centuries. By the 15th century, Trung Trac was even venerated as a goddess of agriculture who protected her people from floods and other natural disasters.[6]

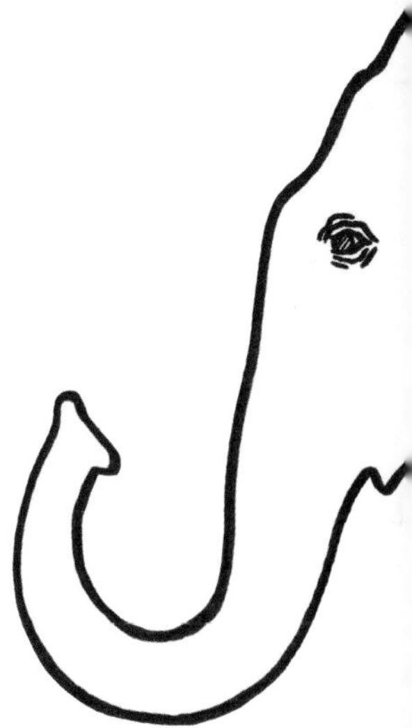

Today, the sisters are celebrated in Vietnam as icons of national pride – a symbol of the country's unceasing resistance to oppression and occupation in its long fight for independence. One unknown 15th-century Vietnamese poet wrote in praise, "All the male heroes bowed their heads in submission / Only the two sisters proudly stood up to avenge the country."[7]

omyris (5th century BC) was an ancient warrior queen of the Massagetae, a nomadic tribe that is believed to have ruled the wild and open plains north of the Amu river in Central Asia and east of the Caspian Sea. Most of what we know of the Massagetae is passed down from the ancient Greek historian Herodotus, who praised their warlike intelligence and the cunning of their queen, and Tomyris is also mentioned by the Macedonian author and military strategist Polyaenus. But although Tomyris does not figure greatly in tales of the ancient world, she is thought to have felled one of its greatest leaders: Cyrus II of Persia, known as Cyrus the Great.

During the time of Tomyris' rule, the Persian emperor had conquered almost every country within reach of his palace, including Babylonia and Phoenicia. Boldly proclaiming himself "king of four quarters of the world",[8] Cyrus set his sights on expanding the northeastern border of his empire, which butted up against Massagetae land. Tomyris had ascended the throne after her husband had died, so Cyrus sent envoys to dangle the offer of marriage. She declined, knowing full well that Cyrus only had conquest on his mind. Her people were free to roam the steppes on their horses, and lived off the plentiful fish in their country and the milk from their herds; they worshipped the sun as their god and wanted for nothing. What would they have got out of subjugation to an avaricious empire-builder?

His nuptial offer spurned, Cyrus decided to advance his territory in the old-fashioned way: invasion. As his troops marched toward the Massagetae, Tomyris sent a sharp warning to the emperor: "King of the Medes, cease to

press this enterprise, for you cannot know if what you are doing will be of real advantage to you. Be content to rule in peace your own kingdom, and bear to see us reign over the countries that are ours to govern."[9]

Of course, Cyrus wouldn't have conquered all the kingdoms in his empire if he backed down easily. When he was deliberating his next move with his closest advisors, Croesus – a Lydian king turned counsellor in the Persian court – warned the emperor that he was not nearly as immortal as he imagined himself to be. However, Croesus also reasoned, "Were it not disgrace intolerable for Cyrus, the son of Cambyses, to retire before and yield ground to a woman?"[10] On Croesus' advice, Cyrus instead hatched a plan to trick Tomyris' army by taking advantage of their unfamiliarity with alcohol.

Cyrus and his army pushed into Massagetae territory and set up camp near the river that marked the border of their land. Leaving behind his worst soldiers and an exquisite feast of fine dishes and wine, he fell back with the rest of his troops and waited. As Croesus had predicted, Tomyris' army descended on the camp and slaughtered everyone in sight. If the Massagetae had been a little more suspicious of the ready-made banquet awaiting their victory, their fate might have been very different. Instead, they gorged themselves on food and dozed off into a booze-addled slumber. This was the cue for Cyrus' army to strike. They annihilated the unwary soldiers and took many hostages – among them Tomyris' own son, Spargapises. (In an alternative version of the story, Polyaenus attributes this sleight-of-hand stratagem to Tomyris herself, and Cyrus' troops are the ones butchered thanks to their love of wine.)

Tomyris was incensed by Cyrus' underhanded scheme, which to her smacked of dishonour and treachery. She sent a messenger to Cyrus, sneering at his use of this unknown "grape juice" in lieu of actual combat: "It was this poison by which you ensnared my child, and so overcame him, not in fair open fight…Restore my son to me and get you from the land unharmed…Refuse, and I swear by the sun, the sovereign lord of the Massagetae, bloodthirsty as you are, I will give you your fill of blood."[11]

Cyrus had no intention of releasing her son until the queen capitulated to him. But events quickly spiralled out of Cyrus' control – Spargapises killed himself in captivity, perhaps recognizing that he would rather die honourably than end up being used as a political pawn against his own mother. Now Tomyris, having exhausted all routes of diplomacy, had reason to unleash the fury of her army on the Persian king.

Gathering up the rest of her forces, she engaged Cyrus in a battle so ferocious that Herodotus reckoned it to be the "fiercest"[12] of all the clashes between the so-called "barbarian"[13] (non-Greek) tribes. Combat began with a thunderous volley of arrows on either side and then both armies were unleashed on each other. The Massagetae were skilled warriors, dressed in magnificent gold and brass, who were just as comfortable on horseback as on foot – and after a prolonged battle on the steppes led by their vengeful queen, they were the ones who finally emerged triumphant. Tomyris scoured the battlefield for Cyrus' body and, upon finding it, made good on her promise to the erstwhile king. Filling a skin with the blood of the slain, she plunged his head into it and proclaimed, "Thus I make good my threat, and give you your fill of blood."[14]

hawlah bint al-Azwar (7th century AD) is one of many Muslim women warriors in Islamic history, though she is also one of its most impressive. In AD 634, Arab forces led by the Muslim warrior Khalid ibn al-Walid rode out in battle to meet no less than the full military might of the Byzantine Empire. They were determined to liberate Syria from the clutches of the Byzantine emperor Heraclius, charging him with the crime of *zulm* (meaning cruelty and oppression) in his governance of the former Roman province. It was going to be a fight to the death, and Khalid's side looked like it was losing.

Heraclius had rallied 200,000 soldiers from all four corners of the empire – troops came from as far away as Armenia, Mesopotamia and Greece – and their tactics were mercenary. The Greek soldiers had chained themselves together, ensuring a bloodbath: nobody could leave the battlefield.

As Khalid's troops uselessly attempted to fall back, a strikingly tall warrior dressed in black galloped through their ranks and sliced through the Byzantine forces, striking down any enemy soldiers in the way. The mysterious knight was soon joined by three more Arab warriors on horseback; one of them grabbed the decapitated head of a Greek fighter, swinging it aloft like a victory banner. Khalid's forces quickly fell into line and dove back into the fray, eventually driving away the Byzantines. When the commander caught up with the saviour of his men, he asked to know the mysterious Black Knight's name.

"I am Khawlah bint al-Azwar al-Kindiyya, sister of Dhiraar ibn al-Azwar and descendant of Arab kings," the warrior replied, drawing back the cloak that hid her face. "I only avoided you out of modesty, for I am a woman of rank and honour. I came to you

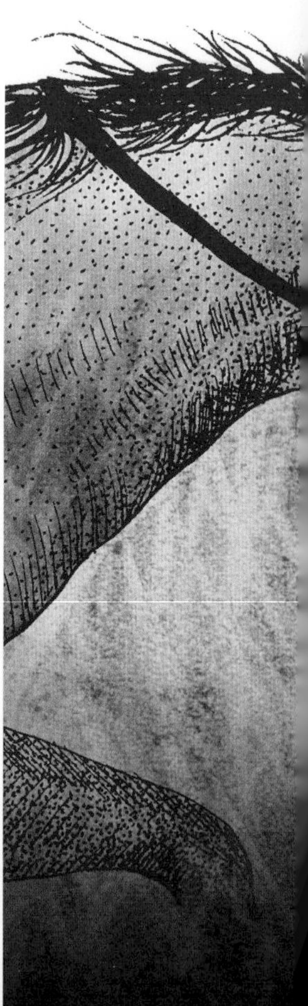

with the Arab women to strengthen you in your fight."[15] Her three captains showed their faces: they were all women, too.

The Qur'an does not forbid women from drawing their swords next to men on the battleground – it was, after all, a female convert named Nusaybah bint Ka'ab who shielded the Prophet Mohammed during the fearsome Battle of Uhud in AD 625. In tribal traditions, Arab women would act as field generals, battle queens and soldiers alongside men – they would also be found at the head of an army, taunting the soldiers and singing to inspire them to greater heights of military valour.

It is thought that Khawlah was one such Bedouin battle queen. Even after she married Mohammed's close relative Ali ibn Abi Talib, she rejected the idea of living in his household.[16] Instead, she and her captains practised camel- and horseback-riding and weaponry every day, continuing to ride at the front of Muslim armies and leading them against the Byzantines.

In one fight, Khawlah and her female forces were surprised in battle and taken prisoner by enemy troops. Confined in a tent and with their weapons gone, her captains began to lose faith, but Khawlah inspired them to fight their way out with nothing more than the tent pegs holding their temporary prison together.

We know little about Khawlah's later life or family, but it is said that Khawlah was "more ferocious than the rain cloud over the Yemen".[17] She is remembered as one of Islam's greatest female warriors and has inspired the names of military academies and girls' schools across the Middle East.

During Japan's Sengoku ("Warring States") period, bloodshed and warfare ruled the land. The bloody civil war spanned from the 15th and 17th centuries and claimed many lives – including, according to some accounts, that of the husband of **Mochizuki Chiyome** (*c.* 16th century). The samurai lord's wife had an unusual way of dealing with grief: founding training school for female ninja.

Little is known about Chiyome's background and her existence is disputed by academics, who query her husband's death and the authenticity of historical documents on her life. Other writers believe that after her spouse's death, Chiyome came under the custody of her uncle-in-law, the powerful feudal lord and military leader Takeda Shingen. His clan controlled the landlocked Kai province and was well known for his use of ninja.[18]

Putting aside the semi-mythic cliché of the flying assassin with near-magical fighting skills, ninjas (also known as *shinobi*) were usually mercenaries for hire, well trained in the art of subterfuge, arson, intelligence gathering and – if necessary – murder. Ninjas were more likely to break into houses and eavesdrop on conversations than to swoop into someone's house and garrotte them. But every war runs on information, and during the warring Sengoku period (*c.* 1467–*c.* 1603) ninja skills were in great demand. Takeda needed to build a network of spies and informants who could extract information and he reasoned that girls and young women were especially suited to the task, as they were less likely to arouse suspicion than their male counterparts.

It is thought that Chiyome established, on Takeda's request, one of the first centres for *kunoichi* ("female ninja"). She began to build an underground cell that could assist her clan in the war effort – and she had plenty of potential recruits to choose from. Thanks to the turmoil of the

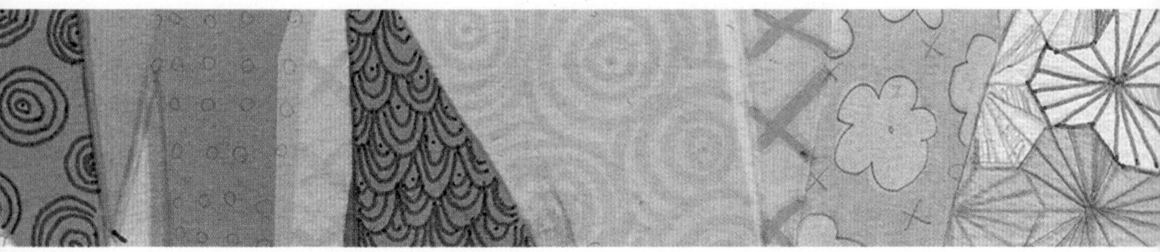

ongoing war, there were many young women who were barely scraping by on the margins of society – orphaned girls, prostitutes, runaways and those who had lost their homes or were abandoned by their families.

Chiyome enticed willing parties to her newly established *kunoichi* academy in the village of Nazu. To outsiders, she must have appeared as a charitable do-gooder assisting those in need, but she was secretly training her young wards in the dark arts of espionage – including intelligence gathering, how to craft disguises and cover stories, and how to transmit messages in code. Some girls were camouflaged themselves as *miko*, Shinto holy women who wandered the country performing religious rituals.

It was the perfect front for a spy who needed to cover large distances and gather information from locals. Whether it was as shrine maidens, actresses or prostitutes, Chiyome's spies spread across enemy territory feeding vital information back to Takeda's forces. It was tough, unglamorous, unappreciated work. The *Bansenshukai* – a guiding text on the art of ninja by 17th-century author Fujibayashi Sabuji – acknowledges the necessity of *kunoichi* while simultaneously deriding them: "When it seems difficult for…male ninja to infiltrate, use [*kunoichi*]. In general, *kunoichi* have a twisted and inferior mind, shallow intelligence and poor speech… you should not use those you cannot follow up."[19]

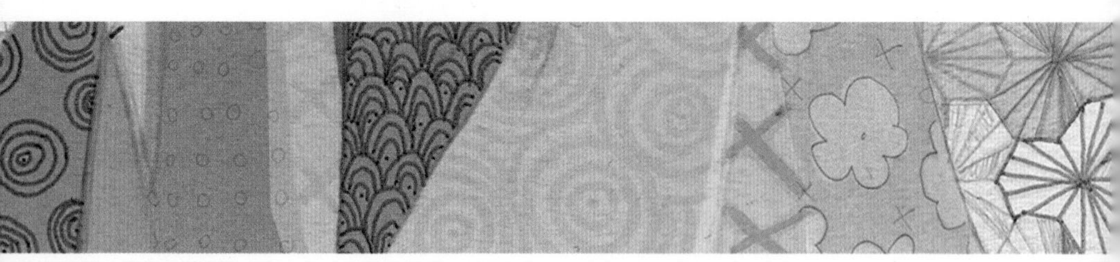

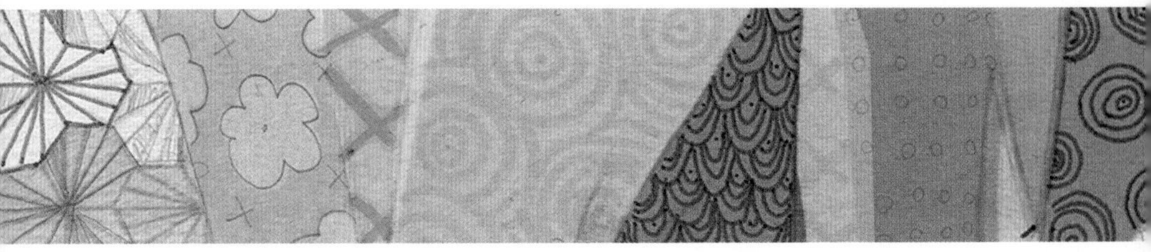

Fujibayashi, however, also notes that *kunoichi* are highly useful when it comes to seducing high-ranking men. But the life of a *kunoichi* was also liable to be cut short, and in one example, Fujibayashi says that a ninja attempting to win the trust of an enemy lord should use a female ninja as a decoy wife, to be held as hostage by the lord in exchange for the fulfilment of the ninja's duties. The deception had a cost, of course – and it was usually the life of the *kunoichi* upon the lord's discovery of the ruse.

Whether or not Chiyome and her school of spies existed at all is still a matter of historical debate, though Takeda was well-known for his use of ninja and Fujibayashi is absolutely clear that *kunoichi* did exist. Many records and ninja manuals from that time languish in the private collections of collectors or in the depths of museum archives, and the very nature of the ninja implies nothing less than secrecy itself. Either way, Takeda's spies were not enough to ensure his victory. In 1573, he died – some say of pneumonia, others claim a single bullet was responsible – and it marked the end of his clan's rise to power. The next recorded instance of a woman leading a ninja school occurs during the later Edo period, sometime between the 17th and 19th century. Fittingly enough for someone who devoted her life to the art of disappearing, Chiyome's ultimate fate – and those of her students – is completely unknown.

n the days before her death, the Chinese feminist poet and revolutionary **Qiu Jin** (1875–1907) wrote a simple poem: "Autumn wind, autumn rain, fill my heart with sorrow."[20] It would be her last words before her execution as a traitor to her own country.

Born in 1875 to an upper class family, Qiu Jin was married off as a young woman to a wealthy Hunanese merchant. In many ways, she was the perfect Chinese wife – she bore two healthy children and even had the bound "lotus" feet that had been so desirable for hundreds of years. But one day in June 1904, Qiu Jin pawned all her jewellery, unwrapped the bandages that constricted her feet and sailed for Japan, leaving her astonished family behind. She was heading into unknown territory, but her experiences over the past few years had driven her to take drastic measures.

While living in Beijing with her family, Qiu Jin had witnessed the terror of the Boxer Rebellion and the humiliating occupation and ransacking of the city by foreign troops. She had also

grown increasingly unhappy with her tyrannical husband; his behaviour, she later wrote, was "worse than an animal's"[21] and was "devoid of virtue".[22]

Escape seemed like the only option, and Japan was home to a growing community of Chinese exiles and students concocting schemes for revolution. Qiu Jin grew convinced that replacing China's weak and ineffectual Qing dynasty rulers with a republican government was the only way for the country to regain its former glory – and that women had to be on the frontline of that battle.

"Equality between men and women is endowed by Heaven," she wrote in a poem entitled "Promoting Women's Rights". "How can we be content to lag behind?...Our fair hands are needed in order to recover our rivers and mountains...We citizen heroines must never fail to live up to our expectations."[23]

In Tokyo, she joined revolutionary groups and began to publish poetry and prose in anti-Qing journals. But Qiu Jin was also intent on carving out a new identity as a warrior woman. Not content with unbinding her feet, she enrolled in rigorous physical education classes and, like her hero, the legendary female warrior Hua Mulan, began dressing in masculine clothing. She even took a second name, Jin Xiong (Chinese for "able to compete with men"[24]) and trained in archery and sword fencing at a martial arts academy. "I am tough and healthy,"[25] she wrote proudly to her brother from Tokyo.

In 1906 Qiu Jin returned to China ready for action. She founded *Chinese Women's Journal* – a publication now recognized as one of China's first feminist magazines[26] – as a clarion call for women to emancipate themselves. "Feet bound so tiny, hair combed so shiny; tied, edged, and decorated with flowers and bouquets," she wrote of women's existence in China. "We spend our lives only knowing how to rely on men – for everything we wear and eat we rely on men."[27]

The journal ran for only two issues, but within it Qiu Jin laid out the foundations of her political thought: men and women were born equal, but her countrywomen were oppressed by their lack of schooling and traditional practices like arranged marriage and foot binding. The only way to overthrow these evils, she reasoned, was to seek a modern education and earn an independent income – as she had done all those years earlier.

As the head of Datong Normal College in the coastal city of Shaoxing, Qiu Jin attempted to translate her thinking into practice. The coeducational school had been set up to educate children in modern subjects like English and physical education, but it had become a front, too, for radical activity – its students were trained in weaponry and other military skills in preparation for the coming rebellion. Qiu Jin, galloping around town on horseback and dressed in men's clothing and Western leather shoes, became a perfect example of the revolutionary forward thinking for her female students.

With her cousin, Xu Xilin, Qiu Jin soon hatched a plot to overthrow imperial rule once and for all, beginning with the assassination of Qing officials in nearby provinces. She even went as far as designing the uniforms for an army-in-waiting: white turbans and black jackets decorated with the Chinese symbol for glory. She imagined the troops riding into battle behind a flag emblazoned with the word *Han* ("Chinese").[28]

But the plan was soon uncovered. Qiu Jin was warned that her arrest was imminent, but she refused to abandon her school. In a letter to a friend, she wrote of her "determination to die for the revolutionary cause".[29] She was apprehended by no fewer than 400 Qing soldiers and brought into custody. At the age of 31, this would-be warrior was beheaded on the grounds of treason. In the wake of her death, even the phrase "physical education" was banned – as thanks to Qiu Jin, it had come to signify revolution. For a woman who had transformed herself from a meek wife with bound feet into a warrior, there could have been no greater compliment.

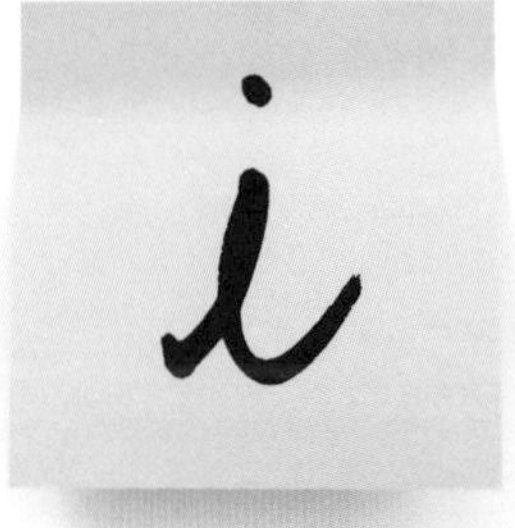

n 1908, the suffragettes had a problem. The campaign for votes was going well – 300,000 people had shown up to a mass rally in London's Hyde Park in June – but they faced increasing aggression from the public and the police. Members of Emmeline Pankhurst's group, the Women's Social and Political Union (WSPU), were routinely arrested – Pankhurst's own daughter, Christabel, was imprisoned in 1905 – and some civilians were also growing hostile to their cause. At a rally in Reading, Berkshire, one man even leaped on stage and knocked out a suffragette.

Enter **Edith Margaret Garrud** (1872–1971). This diminutive woman from the Welsh valleys, believed to be one of the first female martial arts teachers in the West, stood at 150cm (4ft 11in) but had no difficult tossing an 83kg (13-stone) police officer over her shoulder.[30] And it was Edith who taught the same skills to the suffragettes, even training a league of female guards to protect Emmeline Pankhurst.

"Woman is exposed to many perils nowadays, because so many who call themselves men are not worthy of that exalted title, and it is her duty to learn how to defend herself," she noted in *Health and Strength* magazine. "A woman who knows ju-jutsu [ju-jitsu], even though she may not be physically strong...is not helpless."[31]

Edith and her husband, William, had been introduced to ju-jitsu at a demonstration at the Alhambra theatre in London several years earlier. As fitness enthusiasts and physical education teachers, the pair had been so impressed by the sport that they immediately signed up as students. They sped through the course and eventually ended up running a dojo (martial arts hall) in London's Golden Square, where Edith taught special classes for women and children.

The suffragette cause didn't just draw Edith's attention – she also believed that it was wrong that these women were being attacked for their beliefs. On two nights every week, she offered self-defence classes to suffragettes, drilling them in the fine art of excruciating wrist-locks and shoulder throws. The press caught wind of the training sessions and invented a nickname for her students: jujutsuffragettes. Soon, the classes became so popular that Edith had to rent a new room and set up her own dojo in London's Soho district. It even provided a safe haven for any window-smashing protesters fleeing police; they would run to Edith's studio during a demonstration and conceal any incriminating evidence under the mats and floorboards.[32]

"Physical force seems the only thing in which women have not demonstrated their equality to men," she mused in an essay for the suffragette publication *Votes for Women*, "and whilst we are waiting for the evolution which is slowly taking place and bringing about that equality, we might just as well take time by the forelock and use science, otherwise ju-jitsu."[33]

A few months later, Edith was holding public ju-jitsu shows with some 30 suffragettes to resounding applause, repeated curtain calls, and more than a few requests for autographs. In just a few seconds, she would disable men twice her size. She even felled a *Daily Mirror* journalist who requested a demonstration (he later wrote that he "crawled painfully away, pitying the constable whose ill-fortune it should be to lay hands on Mrs Garrud").

Then came Black Friday in 1910. A 300-strong group of suffragettes marched on Parliament to demand an audience with the prime minister. They were met with brutal violence from truncheon-wielding police officers; women were shoved to the ground and trampled underfoot, or picked

up and hurled into groups of male onlookers, where they were groped and fondled. No fewer than 115 protesters were arrested, and two later died of their injuries.

It became obvious that simply teaching small groups of women self-defence was not going to be enough. By 1913, the British government enacted a law, commonly referred to as the Cat and Mouse Act, to trap hunger-striking suffragettes in a vicious cycle of arrest – once a hunger striker released from prison on grounds of ill health had recovered, the police would re-arrest her, effectively keeping her in indefinite detention. It was imperative that the leaders of the movement remain on the streets to rally support for the cause, so the WSPU created The Bodyguard – an underground cell of women tasked with protecting the leaders of the movement from this police harassment.

Edith, of course, was asked to be their ju-jitsu teacher. She trained them in secret, teaching them to hide wooden

clubs under their dresses and use them against any possible assailants, and instructing them in the fine art of trickery. At one rally, officers triumphantly carted off a veiled Emmeline Pankhurst after a skirmish with The Bodyguard – only to realize, on unveiling her, that the women had tricked them with a decoy.

The Bodyguard protected Emmeline until it was dissolved on the advent of World War I. In 1918, the Representation of the People Act was passed, and some women were given the right to vote – but it would be another ten years before universal suffrage was introduced. Yet Edith never forgot her training. She continued to teach classes into her fifties, and even demonstrated a wrist-lock on a journalist who had come to interview her on her 94th birthday. "It is the mind which really has control," she told him, "not only of your muscles and your limbs and how you use them, but also of your thoughts, your whole attitude to life and other people."[34]

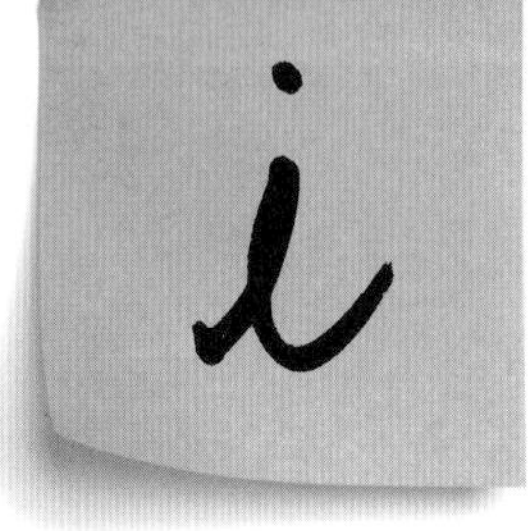

t wasn't unusual to see a woman sailing the high seas at the start of the 19th century – but a female buccaneer leading a military-style confederation of 40,000–60,000 pirates was a much rarer sight. Yet that was exactly what **Ching Shih** (1775–1844), also known as Cheng I Sao, did.

Little is known about Ching Shih's origins, and much of her story has been embellished over time. Historians believe that Ching started out as a prostitute at one of the many floating brothels that dotted the shoreline of Canton in present-day Guangzhou, which was home to opium dens, gambling parlours and other dens of iniquity. In 1801, the 26-year-old Shih married Cheng I, the scion of a fearsome pirate dynasty that had been terrorizing the seas since the late 17th century.

Shih and Cheng's union could not have come at a better time for pirates looking to make their fortune. Since 1792, pirate junks – Chinese ships notable for their elaborate, fan-like sails – had multiplied among the waves. In nearby Vietnam, peasant farmers who sought to overthrow corrupt dynastic rule were not averse to hiring Chinese pirates as privateers to boost their forces. For many impoverished fishermen, a life of crime was preferable to a miserable existence subsisting off their daily catch. But, when the Tay Son rebellion disintegrated in the summer of 1802, their newly organized mercenary army-for-hire was sent back to Cantonese shores. They needed a new leader and a cause to get behind – a power vacuum of which Shih and Cheng were more than happy to take advantage.

They reorganized all the various junks and pirate crews into a federation of ships that was later divided under six coloured flags. At its height, the enterprise totalled 1,600 junks and thousands of men. It was more than a fleet; it was a military organization. This was the venture that Shih inherited by proxy when Cheng unexpectedly died in 1807. Before his death Cheng had adopted Chang Pao, a young fisherman's son, as his apprentice. Shih appointed the young man as the head of the strongest fleet – the Red Flag – and then took him as her lover. Their later marriage strengthened her hold over Cheng's empire even further.

If anybody raised an eyebrow at her unconventional marital arrangements, Shih would likely have cracked down on them with the full power of the law – her law, that is. Shih developed an existing pirate code into a system of laws and bureaucracy, with harsh punishment meted out to whoever fell short of it. She even created a sophisticated system for dividing up booty, and laid out strict rules on the treatment of female captives: a pirate who raped a prisoner would be put to death, while any pirate who took one as his wife and cheated on her would also be executed.

Shih's pirates created a protection racket that stretched down the coastline, and ensnared fishing and trading rigs alike. Protection documents were supplied to those who paid a fee, and those who baulked at the price would be liable to find their ships raided. The enterprise was so successful that it even necessitated the construction of payment offices on land to keep the money flowing in. The pirates operated with full impunity – they destroyed almost half of Canton's official fleet and executed the provincial commander-in-chief when he sailed in for a visit. The Qing government grew desperate and even turned to the British and Portuguese to borrow foreign ships loaded with cannons and soldiers. But these expensive loans were no match for Shih's forces, and Qing officials opted for negotiations – if they could not capture Shih, they could at least seek to compromise with her.

Of course, **Shih was not about to be outgunned at the bargaining table.** In 1810, she disembarked and headed to the Canton governor-general's headquarters to parlay for the best possible deal for herself and her pirates. She was incredibly successful: the government offered her men full amnesty. Those who volunteered themselves were able to keep all their loot and were even appointed to high-ranking positions in the imperial military – Chang Pao was made the lieutenant-colonel of an army regiment and permitted to retain 20 or 30 ships for his private use. As for Shih, she retired into relative anonymity in Canton and never hit the high seas again – although she never lost her taste for the more wicked things in life: when she died at the age of 69, she was the head of a notorious gambling house.

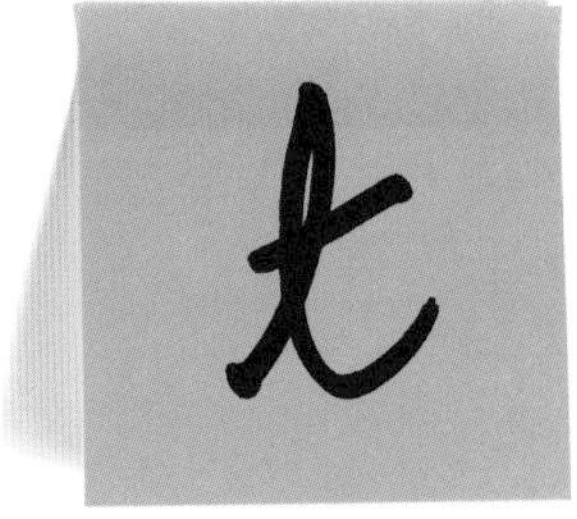

There are few women in antiquity who can claim to have stoked the creative imagination of everyone from Chaucer to Catherine the Great. Cleopatra is one obvious contender, but **Zenobia** (AD 240–unknown) is a more unlikely choice, though just as inspiring. This Arab queen of Palmyra – a woman who single-handedly challenged the authority of the Roman Empire – inspired poets, artists and political leaders for centuries before falling out of common knowledge. Her chastity was praised in *The Canterbury Tales*, her portrait was exhibited in 1878 at the Royal Academy of Arts in London, and in 1897 the Duchess of Devonshire appeared in an elaborate Zenobia costume at a society costume ball.[35]

Zenobia was born in Palmyra, an oasis city in what is now Syria. It was already part of the Roman Empire by the time Zenobia married Odaenathus, Palmyra's widowed and middle-aged Roman commander, and bore him a son. Palmyra had grown independently rich, thanks to its command over silk trading routes from the East. Its cosmopolitan streets heaved with traders and merchants, and their camels, elephants and Arabian horses, all jostling for space in the cool shade of its magnificent temples and fountains. It was the perfect place to launch a new empire – a feat that Zenobia would attempt once Odaenathus was assassinated around AD 267.

Odaenathus and Zenobia's son, Vaballathus, was too young to rule. With the support of the Palmyrene elite, Zenobia took over as queen regent – and she outlasted no fewer than two successive Roman emperors before finally being bested by Aurelian. She liked to compare herself to the Assyrian queen Sammu-ramat (*see* page 140)[36] and claimed affinities with Cleopatra the Great and Dido, Queen of Carthage. Zenobia built a splendid court of intellectuals and military advisors, attracting learned Greek scholars like Longinus, the teacher-turned-counsellor thought to have encouraged Zenobia's empire-building ambitions.

In late AD 269, Zenobia commanded her trusted general Zabdas to attack Egypt, annexing the Roman province of Arabia on his way. The Roman governor of Egypt was away on a military mission, and a usurper called Timagenes was leading an Egyptian revolt. With Zenobia's forces, Timagenes and Zabdas easily seized Egypt from under Rome's nose. When the governor returned, he successfully drove Zenobia's troops out of his territory but made the fatal mistake of attempting to occupy a mountain blocking the Palmyrenes' return to Syria. Thanks to Timagenes' knowledge of the land, however, the opposing army was outpaced by Zenobia and decimated at the summit.

By this point, attitudes in Rome toward Palmyra had hardened. Egypt was under Rome's direct rule, and an occupation of such an important province was a direct challenge to Rome. When Claudius was declared emperor, senators were said to have visited the Temple of Apollo and chanted in his name, "Claudius Augustus, set us free from Zenobia and from Victoria!" (Much like Zenobia, Victoria was a Gallic leader engaged in her own rebellion against the empire.)

But Zenobia's army was already on the move. Her soldiers rode forth and conquered lands as far away as Ancyra, the Turkish city now known as Ankara. Her mission to establish the Palmyrene Empire seemed unstoppable – until, that is, Claudius died of the plague and was succeeded by Aurelian, the steely military commander responsible for defeating the Goths and Vandals. Aurelian brought the full force of the Roman Empire down on the rebels in his eastern provinces and began to march on Palmyra, taking back every newly conquered territory along the way. Many of Zenobia's cities, fearing the bloodshed to come, simply opened their doors and meekly allowed in Aurelian's forces.

When Zenobia and her army retreated to Palmyra, the Romans laid siege to the city with terrifying military contraptions, such as a gargantuan crossbow used to slingshot iron bolts.[37] Amid this terrifying siege, Aurelian and Zenobia exchanged a furious volley of letters, reported by the *Historia Augusta*.

Though the Latin document is now thought to mix historical with literary fiction, it provides some insight into the military negotiations under way.

"You should have done of your own free will what I now command in my letter," Aurelian writes. "For I bid you surrender, promising that your lives shall be spared."[38] Zenobia refused: "You demand my surrender as though you were not aware that Cleopatra preferred to die a queen rather than remain alive, however high her rank." She promised that reinforcements from Persia were en route, and that her army had the Saracens and the Armenians on its side. "The brigands of Syria have defeated your army, Aurelian," she sneered. "What more need be said?"[39]

Unfortunately, Zenobia did not count on the Armenian forces deserting her and joining the Romans, who welcomed them with open arms. Zenobia fled her besieged city on the back of a camel, hoping to reach Persia – to call for their help, or perhaps simply escape – but she was caught before crossing the Euphrates.

Zenobia's ultimate fate is contested. It is believed that she was put on trial and betrayed her closest collaborators and accomplices in exchange for her life, though some accounts hold that she committed suicide rather than endure subjugation. Others claim that she perished as a prisoner during the arduous journey from Palmyra to Rome, or was simply beheaded upon arrival.

Perhaps the most optimistic – and some say the likeliest – account of her fate involves Zenobia being paraded through Rome's streets as part of Aurelian's military celebrations, before being allowed to retire in Rome, where she married a distinguished Roman. Whatever her fate, Zenobia could not have guessed that her memory would live on to inspire later generations – though as a would-be empress to an empire, it is perhaps a more than fitting tribute.

f all of Africa's pre-colonial empire builders, **Amina of Zazzau** (15th–16th century) is perhaps the most legendary. Scholars are still unpicking truth from legend when it comes to this ancient Muslim warrior queen, but it is generally believed that she governed the Hausa kingdom of Zazzau, in what is now northern Nigeria.

Amina was born to rule. She and her sister, Zaria, were two in a long and established dynasty that uniquely allowed men and women to ascend the throne – and when Amina came to the throne, she did just that. She clearly had a natural inclination toward politics: as soon as Amina learned to crawl, oral tradition holds that the toddler would escape from the palace nursery to the throne room to hear her grandfather hold court.

After the king and his heir died, Amina's mother, Bakwa Turunku, was crowned ruler of Zazzau. But it was her gifted daughter who improved on her parents' legacy – and then some. Over her 34-year reign, she vastly expanded the borders of Zazzau and secured boundless wealth and prosperity for her people. When she turned 16, Amina was appointed *magajiya* ("inheritor" or "successor" in Hausa), a traditional title given to a ruler's daughter or sister, and was later crowned *sarauniya* ("queen"). Her rule marked the beginning of a remarkable age for Zazzau, one of seven Hausa states that dominated the region after the dramatic collapse of the enormous Songhai empire at the end of the 16th century.

Amina, an accomplished military tactician and leader, was highly gifted in the art of war – Zazzau expanded its reach to the south and west, and even down to the banks of the mighty Niger river. Her aggressive policy of military conquest paid off. As the 19th-century *Kano Chronicle*, a record documenting the Haus kings and queens, notes, "Zaria, under Queen Amina, conquered all the towns as far as Kwararafa and Nupe. Every town paid tribute to her."

These tributes were notoriously exacting. The king of the Nupe people in Nigeria reportedly sent her 40 eunuchs and no fewer than 10,000 kola nuts, the caffeine-containing fruit of the kola tree in tropical Africa – the first time such a luxury had been glimpsed in Zazzau. By transforming the neighbouring kingdoms into vassal states, Amina was also able to extend her control of the lucrative East–West trading routes that crisscrossed the country, bringing with them wealth and trading riches.

To protect her newly conquered territory, Amina didn't just rely on her formidable army, resplendent as it was in its chain mail and helmets. To repel invaders, she also built tremendous walled earthen forts, which encircled each of her cities. Remnants of these walls, known as *ganuwar Amina* ("Amina's walls"), stand to this day.

Amina's reign was so successful that the queen appears to have had little use for a husband – it is believed that she never married, though it wasn't surprising that she rejected marital custom. After all, marrying African queens was one noted way for Arab rulers in the north to extend their influence in the continent, as royal succession was passed down from mother to daughter,[40] and Amina was too busy consolidating her empire to allow any interlopers to the throne. Besides, if oral tradition about Amina holds true, she wasn't the type for long-term commitment – the queen apparently celebrated the conquest of each new town by taking a local man as her lover for one night. When morning came and she rode out with her army and on to the next target, the unlucky paramour was beheaded.[41]

When Amina died, women continued to rule Zazzau – as she did not have any children, the throne was inherited by her sister, Zaria. She was remembered by her people as "Amina, daughter of Nikatau, a woman as capable as a man".

hree centuries before Joan of Arc rode into battle after hearing God's instruction, there was an even fiercer warrior queen who toiled in the service of Christianity: **Matilda of Tuscany** (1046–1115), also known as Matilda of Canossa. At a time when medieval Europe was torn apart by a fierce battle between Church and State, the reinvigorated clergy in Rome needed a military champion to challenge the secular leadership of the Holy Roman Empire. Matilda answered the call.

The daughter of the margrave of Tuscany, Boniface III, Matilda became heir to the powerful warlord's territory in Northern Italy. Over the course of Matilda's life, Gregorian reformers, under the auspices of Pope Gregory VII, sought to wrestle independence from the Holy Roman Emperor. They wished to seize control of the papacy and put an end to the practice of the nobility appointing bishops and popes, with all the land and money that came with it.

Matilda's father had had a long-standing feud with the Holy Roman Emperor, Henry III, and when Boniface was assassinated during a hunting trip in 1052, many suspected the hand of the emperor at work. Beatrice of Lorraine, Matilda's capable mother, took control of Boniface's lands, remarried and effectively began to groom Matilda for power. Perhaps Beatrice realized that, as sole heiress to the vast Canossa fortune, Matilda was destined for greater things than an arranged marriage and a lifetime of childbearing.

In 1061, the teenage Matilda made her combat debut at her mother's side as they defended the new pope, Alexander II, against those who challenged his papal authority. A 17th-century account of the battle praised her bravery: "Now there appeared in Lombardy at the head of her numerous

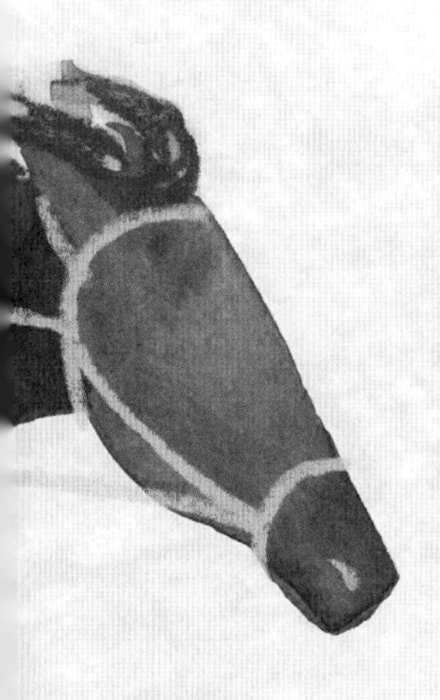

squadrons the young maid Matilda, armed like a warrior, and with such bravery, that she made known to the world that courage and valour in mankind is not indeed a matter of sex, but of heart and spirit."[42]

When Beatrice died in 1076, Matilda inherited a territory that covered all of Tuscany, including important cities like Pisa and Florence, and stretched north of the Alps. More importantly, the route to Rome ran straight through her land. If the forces of the Holy Roman Empire wanted any rebellious clergy in the south, they would have to go through her territory. At the age of 30, **Matilda had become the single most important power broker in the region – and she was on the side of the reformers.**

The new reform pope, Gregory VII, and King Henry IV, who would be crowned Holy Roman Emperor in 1084, had lost none of their predecessors' enmity toward each other. Pope Gregory described Matilda as his "most beloved and loving daughter",[43] and she in return blessed him with the full support of her vast resources. She became one of the few women in medieval history to lead her own troops; it is said that she personally rode with her soldiers into one battle with "the terrible sword of Boniface"[44] and, holding her father's old weapon high, massacred the enemies of the "true pope".

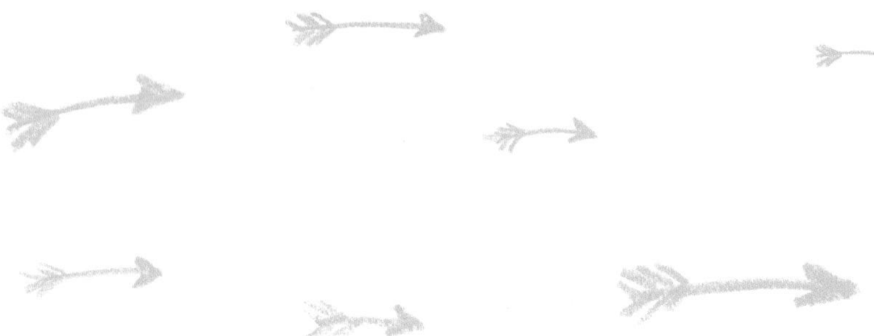

By 1076, Gregory had excommunicated Henry, placing the king in a dangerous position – his subjects could now legitimately seize the throne. Henry was forced to humble himself by travelling to Matilda's castle in Canossa to meet Gregory, standing barefoot in the snow for two days to seek the pope's absolution for his sins. Matilda served as mediator for the two men's uneasy truce, which would break down repeatedly during her lifetime. But wherever the pope was challenged by the emperor and his allies, Matilda and her armies rode out to defend the papacy; their war cry was "For St Peter and Matilda!"[45]

Matilda's warlike devotion to Pope Gregory did not go unnoticed by Henry's supporters. Bishops allied to the king accused the pope, saying, "You have filled the entire Church, as it were, with the stench of the gravest of scandals, rising from your intimacy and cohabitation with another's wife." In furious letters and polemics, Matilda was accused of being a rabid dog "so aroused by female rage that she prefers war to peace".[46]

The *Gran Contessa* may have inherited a certain love of battle from her father (she commanded her last battle when she was in her sixties, no less) but her faithfulness to the Church defined her life – and reshaped the history of Italy. When, toward the end of her life, Matilda commissioned an Italian monk to write her memoirs, she voiced one final assertion of loyalty: "During her life, she gave all her goods to the Church, seeking to empower her as much as she was able; the Church was never betrayed by our Canossa."[47]

n the 12th century, the small Orthodox Christian kingdom of Georgia was poised, literally, at a crossroads. On one side of the country was the Byzantine Empire, and on the other side lay the combined might of the Armenians and Turks. Its people needed a ruler who could unite the country against their neighbouring enemies, and they got it in the form of **Tamar** (*c.*1160–1213) – a medieval queen whose wisdom and military prowess ushered in Georgia's golden age.

"In those times we had nothing but the name of Tamar on our lips; acrostics in honour of the queen were written on the walls of houses; rings, knives and pilgrims' staves were adorned with her praises," wrote one Georgian chronicler of her rule. "Every man's tongue strove to utter something worthy of Tamar's name."[48]

Tamar's ascent to the throne was far from straightforward. Her father, King Giorgi III, was a usurper who had seized the throne from his older brother's son and had him blinded and castrated. Giorgi III may have been cruel, but he adored his child, whom he described as "the bright light of his eyes".[49] When Tamar was 18, he declared her his rightful heir and crowned her co-regent.

The father-and-daughter duo ruled Georgia together for six years. This was unprecedented in the history of Georgia – its language didn't even have a word for queen regnant. But Tamar was naturally gifted at statecraft, and the time she spent at her father's side prepared her well for power.

"Woman though she is, God had created her to be a sovereign. We may say without flattery that she knows how to rule, as indeed we have often remarked among ourselves," declared one Georgian poet, adding, "A lion's cubs are lions all, male and female alike."[50]

When her father died in 1184, Tamar was poised to become the first sovereign queen of Georgia. But she had a potential rebellion on her hands – the all-male feudal elite was none too happy about being ruled by a woman. Though Tamar had already been crowned in her father's time, she had to undergo a second coronation to legitimate her rule, and agree to a marriage arranged by these noble lords, who fully expected her to be content with popping out royal heirs to continue the dynastic line.

They made the dangerous mistake of underestimating Tamar. She was never going to be happy playing housewife in a castle. Three years into her marriage to a hard-drinking Russian prince named Yuri Bogolyubsky, Tamar got fed up with his promiscuity and argumentative ways. She convinced her council to annul the marriage, then she tossed him out of the country. Yuri twice attempted to overthrow his ex-wife with the help of a few mutinous Georgian nobles but was caught by Tamar, and so he failed both times. Tamar could have taken a leaf out of her father's book and done some blinding and castrating of her own, but she chose to exercise a virtue alien to her predecessor: mercy. She simply threw Yuri out of Georgia again and let him retreat to Constantinople.

Yuri wasn't just disloyal; he had proved himself singularly useless in his duties as the provider of the royal seed. Tamar had yet to produce an heir, and so the next time around she opted to select her own husband: David Soslan, a military leader who had helped Tamar win victory over Yuri's troops.

They had a productive partnership in every sense of the word – their marriage produced two children and military conquests that extended Georgia's boundaries farther than ever before. Tamar, skilled at strategy and planning, drew up the plans for battle, and her able husband helped to execute them. The lords who had previously conspired against her were swept up by the excitement of war and fell in line behind their ambitious queen. Tamar led her armies deep into enemy territory, crushing their old enemies on battlefields in present-day Turkey and Azerbaijan, and even as far as northern Iran.

Soon Tamar's reach stretched from the shores of the Black Sea to the Caspian Sea, and the capital, Tbilisi, became one of the biggest and most prosperous cities in the region. When traders exchanged coins on its busy streets, it was Tamar's monogram stamped on them with the words "Queen of Kings and Queens, Glory of the World, Kingdom and Faith".[51] Georgian art and culture bloomed under the hand of this capable queen; Shota Rustaveli, widely regarded as Georgia's greatest poet, wrote the still-loved epic poem *The Knight in the Panther's Skin* and dedicated it to the "jet-haired and ruby-cheeked"[52] Queen Tamar.

By the time Tamar died, she had been Georgia's sole monarch for more than a quarter of a century. But for all her efforts to ensure the future of her kingdom, her hard work came to nothing – within just a few decades of her death, Tamar's heirs would see the kingdom overrun by the Mongol hordes. Nevertheless, for a brief flowering in Georgian history, there was no name sweeter than that of Queen Tamar: "The whole Earth was filled with her praise, she was celebrated in every language wherever her name was known."[53]

The Rulers

Somewhere in the depths of New York City's Metropolitan Museum of Art lie more than ten ancient sculptures depicting **Hatshepsut** (*c.*1508–1458 BC), one of the first women to rule ancient Egypt as a pharaoh. But while the slender curve of her breast and her delicate features are obvious in some of the effigies, others show her in men's attire, with the false beard worn by male pharaohs. There is an additional twist: all the statues are painstakingly reassembled from thousands of tiny fragments. These carvings do not just show Hatshepsut appearing to switch gender – they record the violent erasure of her memory.

Remarkable for being one of the few female pharaohs, Hatshepsut was also one of the most accomplished when it came to reshaping the face of Egypt. Egypt's great builder came to power when her sickly husband, Thutmose II, died, in around 1479 BC. Hatshepsut's stepson and the rightful heir, Thutmose III, was too young to rule, and so she stepped up in time-honoured fashion to rule as regent on his behalf. Seven years in, however, Hatshepsut ditched her title as regent and crowned herself king with a grand coronation on New Year's Day.

While she seems to have pulled off this bold move unopposed, there was still the tricky issue of legitimacy. In true patriarchal fashion, the crown was handed down from father to son – not husband to wife. Scholars believe that this is what prompted her to begin depicting herself as male, or at least to introduce some element of ambiguity into her gender. While inscriptions consistently refer to her with feminine pronouns, she was henceforth commemorated in carvings dressed in the full regalia of a male king and performing all the duties associated with pharaohs. She might not have been of the correct gender to wield power, at least according to Egyptian belief – but she could certainly look the part.

Knowing that it was necessary for her people to believe in the divinity of their rulers, Hatshepsut boldly claimed that she was the result of Amen-Ra – the king of *all* gods – impregnating her mother, Queen Ahmose. After all, who needs to quibble about royal lineage when you can directly trace your ancestry to the gods?

And it appears that she did so successfully, for she lived until around 1458 BC. Over her reign of almost two decades, she embarked on titanic construction projects that reshaped the face of her country. There were gigantic 30m (100ft) obelisks topped with gold, an impressive chapel with red quartzite walls, expansive processional paths between temples for festivals and celebrations, and temple doors of fragrant acacia wood and bronze. Hatshepsut did not spare any expense on her vision.

The mortuary temple at Deir el-Bahari – decorated with wall motifs of her rule and guarded by gigantic statues of Hatshepsut as the Egyptian god Osiris – was perhaps her greatest work. It was meant to guarantee her entry into the afterlife and was intended as the final resting place for both her and her beloved father.

But Hatshepsut's unusual reign was almost obscured in history thanks to her stepson. When Thutmose III ascended the throne after her death, he began to wipe out the most visible and public records that described Hatshepsut as pharaoh. (She was allowed to remain in her lesser role as a queen regent.) In some cases, her likeness and name were chiselled out and written over with the names of her father or brother. Not content with literally rewriting history, Thutmose III is even believed to have disinterred her body, moving it from Deir el-Bahari and reburying it in a more modest tomb with her nurse.

Academics believe that this only began around 20 years into Thutmose III's reign, suggesting that some political development must have made it necessary for him to begin erasing his predecessor from public record – perhaps a worry that Hatshepsut's rule challenged the line of succession.

But Thutmose III failed in his attempt to obliterate Hatshepsut from history. Deir el-Bahari – described as one of the wonders of ancient Egypt – still stands today, hugging the cliffs that line the West Bank of the Nile. In fact, Hatshepsut even seems to have pre-empted the speculation of later Egyptologists that these grand monuments were built by a single woman: "All those who see my monuments in future years," she said, "beware lest you say, 'I know not how this has been done', nor shall he who hears of it say it was a boast – but rather 'How like her this is, how worthy of her father'."[1]

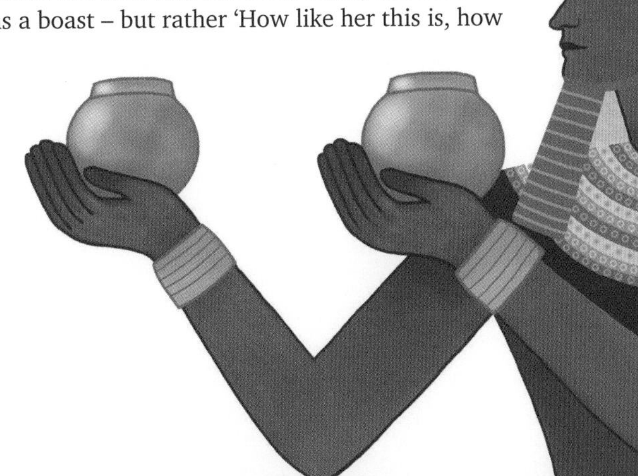

enghis Khan may have been a bloodthirsty despot, but he was also surprisingly enlightened when it came to gender equality. "Whoever can keep a house in order, can keep a territory in order,"[2] the formidable conquerer once declared of Mongol women, who were not shy or retiring by any means. Before his death, Genghis had distributed responsibility for his kingdoms among his four sons and four daughters. Each had power over the various steppe tribes and clans that Genghis had brought to heel as part of his empire. Once Genghis's son Ögodei was crowned Great Khan, however, none of his daughters would come to wield as much power as his daughter-in-law **Töregene Khatun** (unknown–*c.*1241), in her role as the *yeke khatun* – wife of the Great Khan.

Little is known about Töregene's life before her marriage to one of Genghis Khan's powerful sons. Chinese historians trace her lineage to the tribe of herders known as the Naiman, who followed Christianity and roamed across the lush forests of the Khangai Mountains in western Mongolia. The Naiman, like many of the clans and tribes in Mongolia, had pledged allegiance to Genghis after being worn down by his army. Töregene, a tribal princess, was already on her second marriage by the time she wed Genghis's son Ögodei – her first was to the son of a rival chief who belonged to another tribe crushed by Genghis's forces.

Like all of Genghis's sons, Ögodei was a rabble-rousing drunk – in fact, his appointment as Great Khan may have been decided by the fact that he was able to hold his drink better than his other siblings. But his cruelty found other terrifying methods of expression. In 1237, he seized his sister's kingdom of Oirat by subduing its people in the most horrific way possible: by mass rape. Four thousand girls over the age of seven were stripped and raped by Ögodei's soldiers in front of their trembling families as the ultimate display of power. His avaricious 12-year reign was cut short only when he died, in 1241 – possibly as a result of his drinking.

This left Töregene in control of the Mongol Empire, a vast territory that spanned more than 28 million square kilometres (11 million square miles)[3] – a land mass that rivalled the size of Africa. Töregene had previous experience with court administration and palace intrigue: after all, she had already outlived her unfortunate first husband. While Ögodei was alive, she had exercised enormous influence over his affairs, with the power to raise taxes and appoint tax collectors. Now that he was dead, she replaced powerful provincial governors and ministers, such as the chancellor and finance minister, with her chosen favourites.

She also made the unusual decision of appointing a foreign-born Muslim, Fatima, as her closest advisor. Most likely a trophy from a military campaign in the Middle East, Fatima had come to the Mongol court as a captive, part of the spoils of war. Töregene and Fatima had this in common, and the empress repaid their friendship by making her servant her dearest aide. One Persian scribe described her as "the sharer of intimate confidences and the depository of hidden secrets". While more senior ministers were stonewalled by Töregene, Fatima herself was "free to issue commands and prohibitions".[4]

Töregene's consolidation of power was aimed at one thing: ensuring that her son, Güyük, was made Great Khan. She twice called a *kurultai* (an official council) to ratify his election as Ögodei's successor. Töregene had inherited some of her husband's bloodlust, too – she had the provincial governor of eastern Iran put to death by packing his mouth with stones until he suffocated. She also accused Ögodei's sister, Al-Altun, of having poisoned Ögodei and had her executed, too.

Finally, Töregene succeeded in her quest when Güyük was crowned Mongol emperor in an imperial ceremony that drew guests from all the Great Khan's far-off lands. But Güyük proved to be an ungrateful son, and he grew displeased with how much power in the empire Töregene still wielded. Worst of all, he despised his mother's trusted aide, Fatima, and wanted her arrested. Töregene refused to give her up, thus sealing both their fates.

Güyük tortured Fatima for days and forced her to confess that she had bewitched Töregene, before having her drowned. The exact details of Töregene's death are unknown, but it is likely that Güyük also murdered her, thus marking the end of Töregene's short-lived reign as the Mongol Empire's most powerful empress.

Plenty of women in history have been accused of bringing down kings, but none more so than **Brunhilda of Austrasia** (*c.* AD 543–613), the Visigothic princess who was accused of the deaths of ten rulers between the 6th and 7th centuries.

Brunhilda was an unforgiving and tenacious woman. While other royals perished in assassination plots or wars, she staked her claim to power in medieval Europe well into her old age, thrice ruling as queen regent of Austrasia – a sprawling kingdom that covered parts of modern-day France, Germany, Belgium, Luxembourg and the Netherlands.

As a maiden in what is now Toledo, Spain, Brunhilda was praised as "honourable and comely, prudent in judgment, and amiable of address".[5] King Sigebert I of Austrasia saw a good match in the princess. As one of four brothers, all of whom were Frankish kings of their own neighbouring states, he disdained the lowly marriages that some of his siblings had made with women of lesser status and serving maids. His brother Chilperic – king of neighbouring Neustria – followed suit and asked for the hand of Brunhilda's older sister, Galswintha.

But while Brunhilda and Sigebert settled easily into royal matrimony, the same could not be said of Chilperic and Galswintha. Chilperic was still in love with his mistress, Fredegund, even though he had sworn to kick her out of the marital bedchamber once Galswintha arrived. Brunhilda's sister grew unhappier by the day and begged Chilperic to let her return to her father. He rejected this, and she was strangled to death in her bed shortly afterward. Fredegund was installed as queen of Neustria a few days later.

An incensed Brunhilda was certain that Fredegund and Chilperic were behind her sister's murder. Now the queen of Austrasia, she spent the next few decades seeking revenge for her slain sister. Brunhilda

convinced Sigebert to attack his brother, prompting seven long years of war, which was finally brought to a halt when Fredegund sent men to assassinate Brunhilda's husband with poisoned knives. Now Brunhilda and her son, Childebert II, were left completely exposed.

This act of treachery could have sunk Brunhilda's fortunes completely. But she refused to be cowed by the king and queen responsible for the murder of both her sister and her husband. Instead, she persuaded Sigebert's other brother, the childless King Guntram of Burgundy, to adopt Childebert II, securing her child's fortunes in the years to come.

Childebert II inherited Burgundy when Guntram passed away, but Fredegund, now regent of Neustria in the wake of Chilperic's death, was up to her old tricks. Brunhilda's son died unexpectedly in his twenties, and Brunhilda accused Fredegund of poisoning him. But the death of Childebert II did have the convenient side effect of putting Brunhilda in direct power once again – and, this time, she was in charge of two kingdoms.

As regent of Burgundy and Austrasia, she could only hold power until Childebert II's two sons, Theudebert II and Theuderic II, came of age and began to rule each kingdom separately. Two years in, Theudebert II came of age and inherited Austrasia. Perhaps with good reason, he was suspicious of his grandmother and promptly exiled her. She made her way to her younger grandson, Theuderic II, who by then was ruling Burgundy. There, she made her presence known – putting traitors to death, launching assassination plots against Burgundy nobles and worming her way into the heart of power. While Theuderic II was on the throne, Brunhilda was the one calling the shots – a state of affairs made even more evident by the fact that Theuderic II was still a bachelor and lacked an heir even at the relatively advanced age of 20.

Never one to forgive or forget, she also got Theuderic II to imprison his brother and claim the throne of Austrasia – and while Theudebert II was languishing behind bars, she had him assassinated. With all her foes deceased, including the long-dead Fredegund, Brunhilda was now the only one left standing. Less than a year into his rule over the two realms, Theuderic II died of dysentery.

Brunhilda hadn't reckoned with the Franks' distaste for their power-hungry queen regent, which had simmered unchecked ever since her arrival in northern Europe. In fact, her subjects would rather have seen Brunhilda out of power than reigning triumphant. Officials from Austrasia and Burgundy invited Fredegund's son, Chlothar II, to invade Brunhilda's kingdom. The military campaign proved almost too easy, especially after Brunhilda's military leaders deserted her. She was easily captured by Chlothar II, who charged her with murdering ten kings – a largely exaggerated claim that blamed her for the deaths of various high-born men, including that of his father, Chilperic, Brunhilda's grandchildren Theudebert and Theuderic, and even her own husband Sigebert. Baseless or not, medieval historian Fredegar notes that Chlothar was "boiling with fury against her." He continues, "She was tormented for three days with a diversity of tortures, and then on [Chlothar II's] orders was led through the ranks on a camel. Finally she was tied by her hair, one arm, and one leg to the tail of an unbroken horse, and she was cut to shreds by its hoofs at the pace it went."[6]

Brunhilda was around 70 by the time she met her death. While excruciating by any measure, her late demise was also proof of her skill and craftiness. Even as a stranger to the lands in which she found herself, Brunhilda managed to wreak havoc on the lives of all who had double-crossed her – even if it was her old rival's son who eventually deposed her.

rom its birth as part of the Roman Empire to its later conquest by Ottoman Turks, Constantinople (present-day Istanbul) was ruled by a complex web of backstabbing, palace intrigue and lust. The 11th-century Byzantine empress **Zoë Porphyrogenita** (*c.* AD 978–1050) – through marriage and sponsorship – negotiated all three to successfully crown or sponsor no fewer than four men to the throne.

Born as the middle child of Emperor Constantine VIII, Zoë had the brightest marriage prospects of his three daughters. Her elder sister had chosen to enter a nunnery, while her younger sibling, Theodora, was of distinctly plain appearance. Zoë was initially betrothed to Otto III, the heir of the Holy Roman Empire, but this ended in disaster when the prospective groom died while the bride was en route to Italy. Zoë's marital plans were therefore suspended as her father resumed his rule. It was only on his deathbed – by which time Zoë was 50 years old – that Constantine began to cast around for a husband for her. He finally settled on Romanos, the urban prefect of Constantinople.

Their marriage legitimated Romanos as emperor and Zoë as empress. But if Romanos was grateful for his elevation in fortune, he didn't exactly show it. At 50, Zoë was too old to conceive, but Romanos refused to let the matter rest. She obligingly submitted to various fertility-boosting oils and massages,

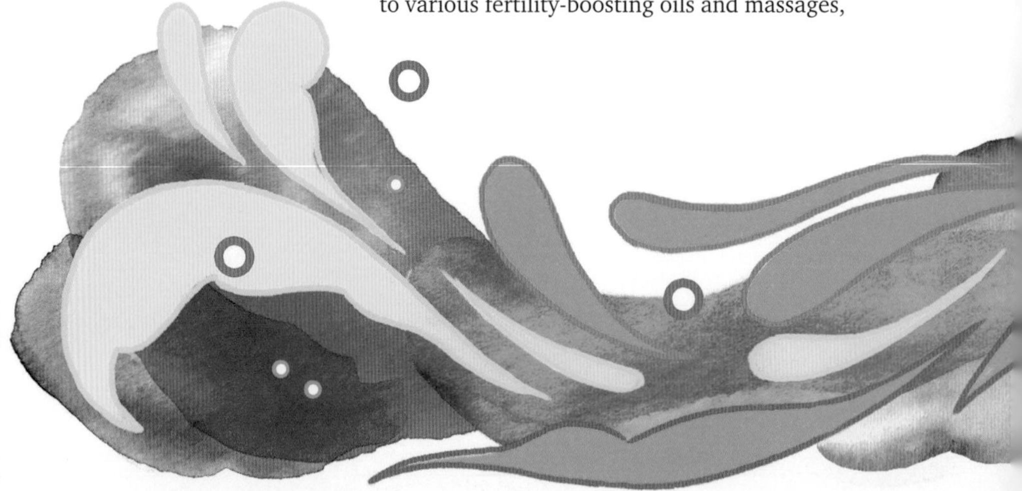

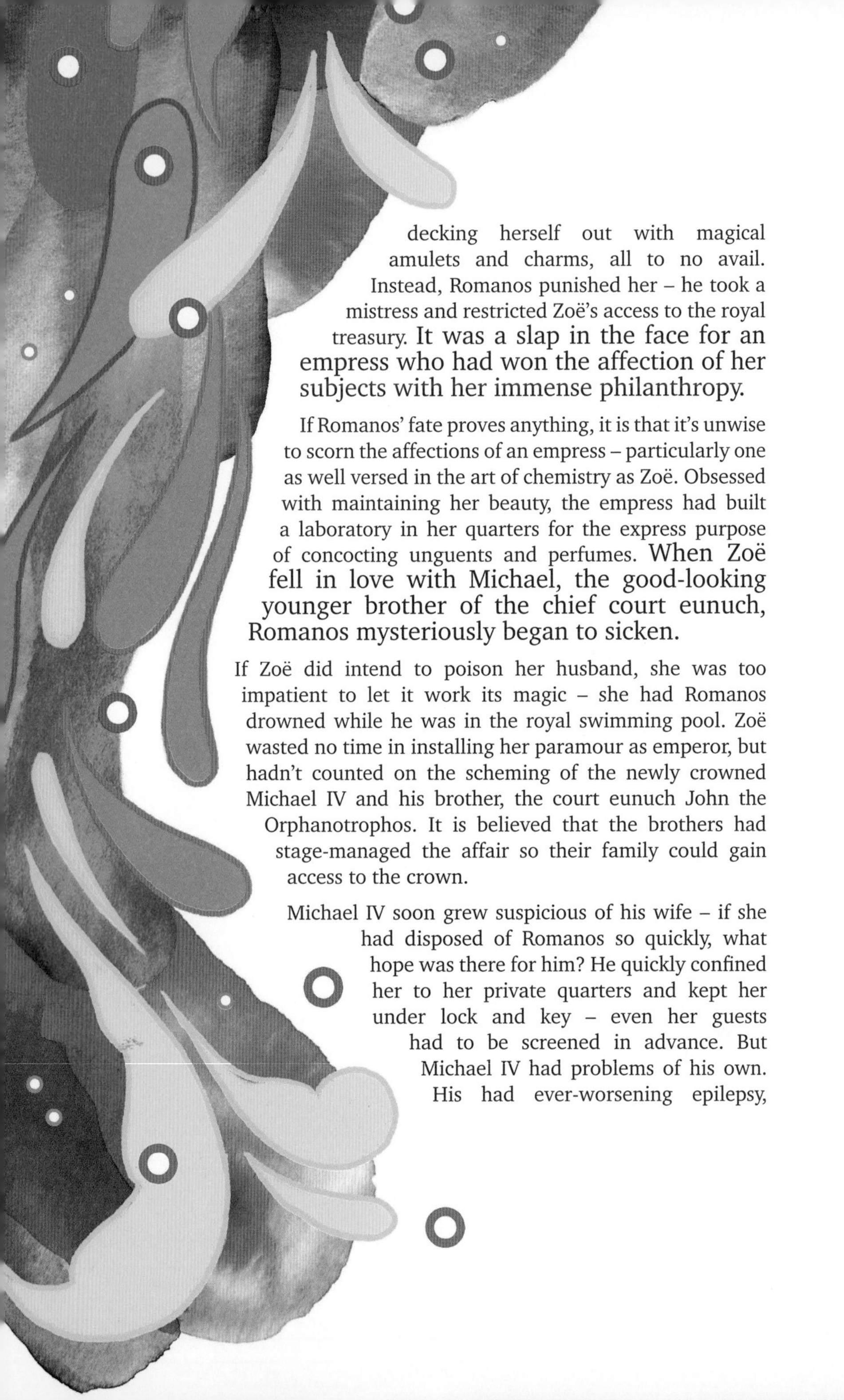

decking herself out with magical amulets and charms, all to no avail. Instead, Romanos punished her – he took a mistress and restricted Zoë's access to the royal treasury. It was a slap in the face for an empress who had won the affection of her subjects with her immense philanthropy.

If Romanos' fate proves anything, it is that it's unwise to scorn the affections of an empress – particularly one as well versed in the art of chemistry as Zoë. Obsessed with maintaining her beauty, the empress had built a laboratory in her quarters for the express purpose of concocting unguents and perfumes. When Zoë fell in love with Michael, the good-looking younger brother of the chief court eunuch, Romanos mysteriously began to sicken.

If Zoë did intend to poison her husband, she was too impatient to let it work its magic – she had Romanos drowned while he was in the royal swimming pool. Zoë wasted no time in installing her paramour as emperor, but hadn't counted on the scheming of the newly crowned Michael IV and his brother, the court eunuch John the Orphanotrophos. It is believed that the brothers had stage-managed the affair so their family could gain access to the crown.

Michael IV soon grew suspicious of his wife – if she had disposed of Romanos so quickly, what hope was there for him? He quickly confined her to her private quarters and kept her under lock and key – even her guests had to be screened in advance. But Michael IV had problems of his own. His had ever-worsening epilepsy, and he and Zoë were unable to produce an heir. Ever the schemer, his brother suggested that Zoë adopt his nephew – another ambitious young Michael – in order to assure the continuation of the dynasty. She was disarmed by their flattery and promises, and was told that Michael V – as he was later crowned – would be emperor in name only. For a woman sequestered away for years, this pledge must have seemed irresistible.

Deceit and cruelty clearly ran in both Michaels' family. In April 1042, Michael V banished Zoë to a monastery. But he hadn't counted on the unusual and dramatic support that Zoë enjoyed among the people of Constantinople, especially its women – in response to his treachery, hordes of people left their homes and took to the streets in righteous protest. The Byzantine historian Psellos records the women in the mob declaring, "Where can she be, she who alone of all women is free...the rightful heir to the Empire? How was it this low-born fellow dared to raise a hand against a woman of such lineage?"[7] Over the course of this three-day riot, the mob tore down the emperor's buildings and bayed for his blood. Finally, Zoë was freed and her captors blinded in front of a mocking public.

After a three-month period, in which she ruled jointly with her sister Theodora, Zoë took a third husband: Constantine IX, a member of the court and an old friend. By this point, Zoë, at 64, had outlasted the scheming men of her court and was clearly going nowhere. When she finally died in her seventies, it was with an outpouring of generosity to the public that had freed her. Psellos writes, "She opened up the imperial treasury and allowed the gold kept there to pour forth like a river. So the gold was squandered with all the uncontrolled profusion of a flood, and Zoë, after a short and painful illness...departed this life at the age of seventy-two."[8]

Pitiable orphan, genocidal murderer, loving mother, tyrannical despot – few monarchs have cycled through as many identities as **Catherine de Medici** (1519–1589). Centuries after her death, this Italian-born queen and regent of France still divides opinion. But one thing is certain – like her better-known contemporary Elizabeth I, Catherine was one of the most powerful women in Renaissance Europe.

Born in 16th-century Florence, Catherine was scarcely three weeks old when her parents died. But the only child of a Medici duke and a French princess would prove a useful pawn for Cardinal Giulio de Medici, her relative and appointed guardian – the man soon to be elected Pope Clement VII. Thanks to her parents' wealth, Catherine was one of the richest heiresses in Europe.[9] When she turned 14, her marriage was arranged to Henry, Duke of Orléans, the second son of King Francis I of France.

The marriage did not get off to a good start. The French were suspicious of this Florentine stranger, the daughter of a common-born merchant, though she tried her best to win them over with her fine wit and manners. But disaster struck a year into the arranged marriage – Pope Clement VII died, leaving her lavish dowry unpaid and diminishing her political status even further in the French court. And there was a second, more pressing problem – Henry was in love with a woman 19 years his senior.

Diane de Poitiers was a widower charged with tutoring Henry, but their relationship soon blossomed into a full-blown affair. Henry was shamelessly infatuated with his mistress; he wore her chosen colours of black and silver everywhere, and stamped their joint initials in gold on all his buildings. It is thought that their affair began sometime after the unexpected death of Henry's older brother, which made Henry and Catherine the future king and queen of France – with Diane lurking in the wings, of course.

Catherine quietly swallowed Henry's infidelity and focused on doing her duty as a queen-in-waiting: childbearing. But no matter how they tried, Catherine could not fall pregnant. She faced the stark possibility of repudiation and divorce – there was no point to the marriage, people reasoned, if Henry's wife could not bear a child. But Catherine possessed an iron will. She tried everything: she drank the urine of pregnant animals, attempted pagan and herbal remedies, and even spied on Henry and Diane's lovemaking to see if she was doing it wrong. Ten years went by until salvation arrived in the form of a doctor called Jean Fernel, who examined both Catherine and Henry, and prescribed a cure that has since been lost to history. Whatever it was, it obviously worked miracles – Catherine would go on to produce nine children, including five boys, cementing her position within the court.

When Francis I died in 1547, Henry ascended the throne. His reign would last only 12 years; on a summer's night in 1559, Catherine awoke from a nightmare in which she saw her husband wounded. She begged him not to take part in an upcoming joust, but her warnings went unheeded. On the day of the competition, a lance smashed into his face, the splinters piercing his eye and brain. Ten days later, he died of infection.

With that, Catherine entered the next phase of her life – as the de facto ruler of France. Her son, the newly crowned Francis II, had been a delicate and sickly child, and easily ceded power to his mother. Catherine was not shy about making her presence known; all of Francis II's decrees started off, "This being the good pleasure of the Queen, my lady mother and I, also approving of every opinion that she holdeth, am content and command that." By December 1560, Francis II succumbed to illness and died. Catherine's next son in line to the throne, Charles IX, was only ten. At the age of 41, Catherine declared herself regent and governed France in his stead. And when Charles IX died of tuberculosis at the age of 23, she would rule as regent for her third son, Henry III.

Catherine inherited a divided country that was facing civil war. The French Catholics were at loggerheads with the ever-growing minority of Protestants, known as Huguenots. The state regarded the Huguenots' reformist faith as heresy, but Catherine skilfully manoeuvred between the two; she engineered the marriage of one daughter to the devoutly Catholic Philip II of Spain and the other to Henry III of Navarre, a Protestant.

It was the latter marriage that would lead to the blackest mark against Catherine's character: the St Bartholomew's Day Massacre in August 1572. Huguenots had poured into Paris to celebrate the marriage of their king, only to witness the attempted assassination of one of their leaders, Admiral Coligny. Within days, a rampaging mob of Catholics had swept through the streets of the city, slitting the throats of any Protestants in sight and tossing their bodies into the river Seine. The violence quickly spread through the rest of the kingdom, claiming some 20,000–30,000 lives.

Huguenot writers placed the blame for the massacre squarely on Catherine's head, though historians now argue that she feared Huguenot retaliation for the mysterious assassination attempt, and so ordered a pre-emptive strike on their leaders – and that she had never intended the political killings to spark riots. Regardless, the legend of the cold-hearted, deceitful Black Queen was born. It did not help that powerful women were regarded with suspicion in the 16th century, especially one so interested in learning and the occult as Catherine. The English pamphleteer John Stubbs smeared her as a witch in league with "familiar spirits" (demons that were believed to assist witches).

But if Catherine was guilty of one thing, it was of undying devotion to her sons. Over the decades, she had used all her cunning and courage to ensure that their kingdom did not disintegrate into civil war, and that their birthright remained unchallenged. But when she died in 1589, the dynasty that she had done so much to protect fell to pieces in a matter of months with the assassination of Henry III. Even so, Catherine – the orphan daughter of a merchant – had still managed to reshape the history of France itself.

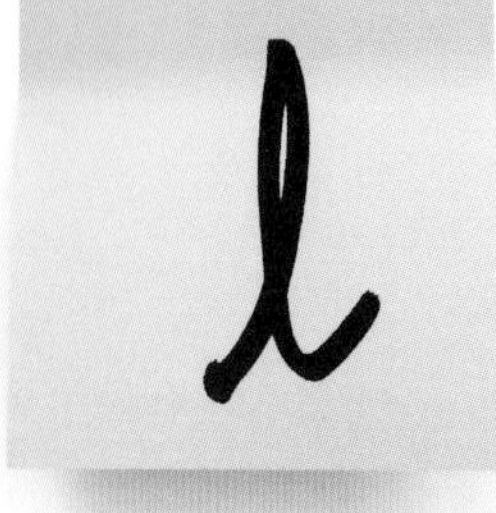

ong before Christopher Columbus "discovered" the Caribbean island of Hispaniola – now home to Haiti and the Dominican Republic – it was the property of the indigenous Taíno people. At the time of the Italian explorer's landing in 1492, Hispaniola was divided into five kingdoms, ruled over by tribal chieftains known as *caciques*, and none would prove as gifted, artistic or adored by their people as **Anacaona** (*c.* 1474–1503).

Anacaona was royal by virtue of both bloodline and marriage. Her brother was Behechio, the *cacique* of Xaragua, a southwestern principality in the island, and she was married to Caonabo, the *cacique* of its neighbouring Maguana.

When Columbus landed in 1492, he quickly realized the potential value of Hispaniola. For one thing, the *caciques* he encountered were draped in gold, and the chiefs' names even incorporated the Taíno word for gold, *caona*, as a sign of status. (Anacaona's name, in fact, translates as "golden flower".) While most of the Taíno welcomed Columbus, it seems that Anacaona's husband soon realized that the explorer's intentions were not as innocuous as they seemed.

When Columbus resumed his voyage around the New World, he left behind 39 sailors on the island to search for gold. The next year, he returned and found the would-be conquerors dead and their settlement burned to the ground. As retribution, the Spanish captured Caonabo and shipped him off to Spain. He died of unknown causes en route.

As a result of Caonabo's death, Anacaona ruled Xaragua as *cacique* alongside her brother. The learned queen was famous for her skills in poetry, song and the arts – her *areytos* (ritual dances) were loved all over the island. She was described by Haitian historian Jean

Fouchard as "queen of language, of ceremony, of games and pleasures".[10]

But the Spanish were seduced by the prospect of gold and profit more than the charming pastimes of the royal court. After establishing a second, more successful settlement on Hispaniola, they began to kidnap and enslave locals to work in their gold mines and on their plantations. War broke out between the conquistadors and the indigenous people. Because the Taíno had no immunity to European disease, illnesses like smallpox and measles ravaged the local population. Facing the prospect of being worked to death in Spanish farms, some Taíno even committed suicide.

By the beginning of the 16th century, the Spanish were bringing the Taíno to heel. Xaragua was one of the last remaining Taíno strongholds, and while its people were not rich in gold, the Spanish still wanted them to pay tribute to the Spanish crown as a demonstration of their loyalty. Columbus's brother, Bartholomew, was sent to extract gifts of cotton and gold from Anacaona and her brother, Behechio. He was welcomed with hospitality – Anacaona gave him gifts of precious cotton and 14 ornately carved seats made of black wood.

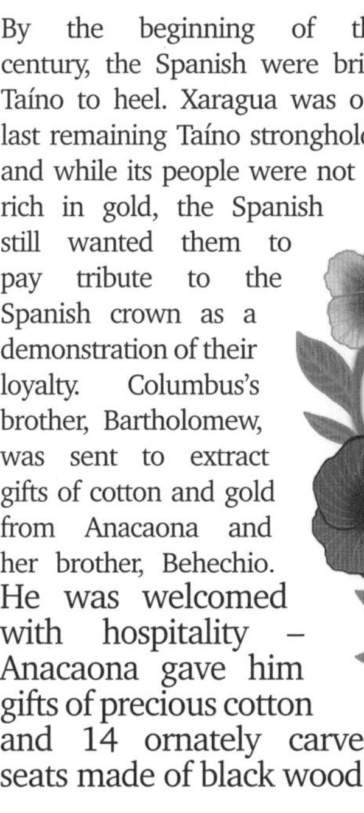

It was this hospitality that may have undone Anacaona. Six years after Bartholomew's visit, Behechio had died, and Anacaona had assumed sole power. Hispaniola governor Nicolás de Ovando came to her kingdom on the pretence of a friendly visit – albeit one accompanied by 300 Spanish infantry and 70 men on horses. The queen, expecting only a diplomatic mission, had invited 32 lesser chieftains to welcome Ovando. After days of feasting and festivities, Ovando enticed Anacaona and her *caciques* to a gathering – some say under the pretext of signing a peace treaty with the Spanish or watching a horsemanship tournament.

It turned out to be a hideous deception: Ovando was intent on subduing one of the last strongholds of Taíno power. When he touched the cross on his chest, his soldiers moved in and massacred the *caciques*. Others were taken into a house, tortured into confessing that Anacoana had schemed against the Spanish, and then burnt to death in the building. Anacaona herself was captured, convicted of treason and hanged in the capital of Hispaniola, Santo Domingo. Without its leader, the kingdom of Xaragua fell apart and was quickly colonized.

In less than half a century, the Taíno would be effectively exterminated by the Spanish through illness, slavery and strife. There is little that remains of their culture or the *areytos* that Anacaona's people loved so much. But Anacaona has become a symbol of resistance and pride for both Haitians and Dominicans – an example of an indigenous queen who ruled her people with grace.

f you ask a person on the street about **Catherine the Great** (1729–1796), it's likely that they will know one of three things: she was a Russian empress, she had numerous love affairs, and she may or may not have had intercourse with a horse.

You can blame posthumous gossip for that last one. Courtesy of her enemies in France, the legend most attached to Russia's longest-serving tsarina is that she died having sex with a stallion – and the story has only grown more elaborate with the passing centuries. (For the record, she actually died of a stroke.)

Catherine's sprawling love life – she is thought to have gone through 21 lovers over 44 years[11] – was often used against her, though her 18th-century body-count now looks rather restrained by 21st-century standards. Her obvious passion for romance and sex has fuelled dozens of biographies, but far less appreciated and discussed is her capability as ruler. In fact, Catherine had political savvy by the bucketload – enough to rise from an impoverished princess to the greatest female ruler that Russia has ever known.

Born in 1729 into the hard-up family of a German princeling, Catherine was summoned from Prussia to St Petersburg by the Russian Empress Elizabeth to marry Grand Duke Peter, Elizabeth's nephew and the future Russian emperor. Her family was so poor that the young woman's dowry consisted of three old dresses and some lingerie. But 15-year-old Catherine knew how to charm her way into the affections of a foreign court;

she threw herself into learning Russian and, against the wishes of her father, converted to the Russian Orthodox Church. A year later, she was married to Peter; their bridal procession was drawn by eight white horses, and there was a diamond-encrusted crown on Catherine's head.

But Peter was either unwilling or unable to fulfil his marital duties. On their wedding night, he passed out after supper without touching Catherine, and, as she writes in her memoirs, "Matters remained in this state without the slightest change during the following nine years." The rejection stung, but it forced Catherine into self-sufficiency. She told herself, "Keep on a leash any affection you might feel for this gentleman; you have yourself to think about, my dear girl."[12]

There was still the problem of providing an heir. Peter, who was more enthusiastic about playing with toy soldiers, was unforthcoming in this respect. Catherine struck up a love affair with Sergei Saltykov, a gentleman-in-waiting, only to miscarry twice. Finally, in 1754, Catherine gave birth on the floor of her chambers and provided the long-awaited son – even if his paternity was in doubt. When Empress Elizabeth died in 1762, and Peter ascended the throne, Catherine began to ponder her own political fortunes. Peter had grown into an incompetent drunk, and factions in court began to ally themselves with her, sensing her to be a safer bet than the royal lush.

The new emperor exasperated and confounded his people in equal measure. He insulted the clergy, initiated a pointless

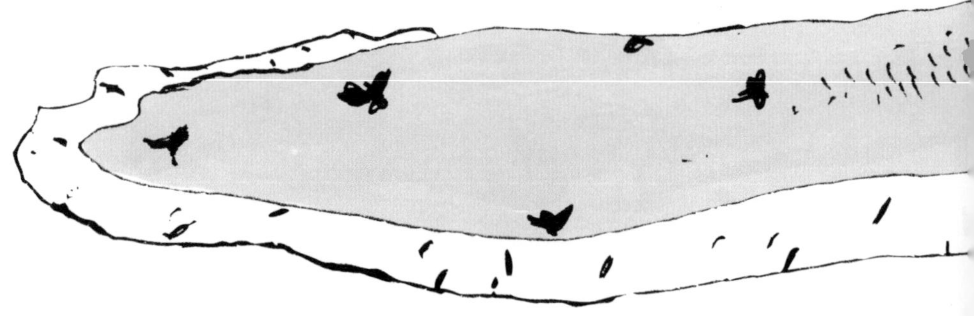

war with Denmark and even signed a disastrous peace treaty with Russia's long-standing enemy, Prussia. Catherine waited patiently for Russia to turn against Peter, and when it did, she overthrew her husband. By July – only six months into Peter's reign – she launched a coup d'état, proclaiming herself *gosudarina* (sovereign autocrat) and her son heir to the throne.

Over her 34-year reign, Catherine not only held on to power but also wielded it brilliantly, with many describing the period of her rule as the golden age of the Russian Empire. Under Catherine, Russian forces established control over the northern shores of the Black Sea. Even her parade of affairs proved useful in this regard; when she raised one talented lover, the military officer Grigory Potemkin, to an eye-wateringly high rank, he repaid her by successfully annexing the Crimea.

Her achievements were not just limited to the military sphere. At home, she also built hospitals, expanded universities and attempted to reform Russian law so that it better adhered to her own values, culled from her voracious reading of Montesquieu and other great thinkers. Though the resulting set of legal guidelines, the *Nakaz*, was never put into practice, it dealt with everything from the administration of justice to principles of religious freedom and introduced Enlightenment principles to Russian government.

By the time Catherine passed away at the age of 67, Russia had been transformed into a global power, the borders of which stretched from Poland to the Crimea. She may never have found a way to marry her Enlightenment ideals with the demands of autocratic rule, but she died leaving her country in a far better place than it had been under Peter.

No woman has ruled Russia since her death. In fact, her son Paul I, who succeeded her as emperor, altered the rules of succession so that men were the preferred candidates – which we can only see as the highest praise for all that Catherine accomplished.

iven the fact that few women were allowed to inherit land or property in medieval Europe – let alone kingship – it seems ludicrous that one woman was allowed to do all three. Even more remarkable is the fact that **Jadwiga** (1373/4–1399), the youngest daughter of Louis the Great, King of Hungary and Poland, managed this hat trick at the tender age of 11.

When Louis the Great passed away in 1382, he died having devised a master plan for Jadwiga and her older sister, Maria. Maria was set to inherit Poland and was engaged to Sigismund of Luxemburg, the son of the Holy Roman Emperor Charles IV; Jadwiga was to take Hungary and marry her childhood companion William of Habsburg, the eldest son of an Austrian duke. Seven days after Louis's death, however, his best-laid schemes were undone when his wife – Jadwiga's and Maria's mother – had Maria crowned as ruler of Hungary and sought to rule Jadwiga's kingdom as regent.

After much to-ing and fro-ing that left Jadwiga with the country originally intended for her sister: Poland. Not a shabby trade-off by any means, but it came with considerable downsides. For one, Jadwiga had spent most of her infancy in Hungary and had little or no relationship with her new kingdom. For another, the Polish nobility demanded that the new ruler had to reside in their country – and if one wasn't sent posthaste, they would simply elect a new one themselves. A young Jadwiga was promptly torn from her family and shipped off to Poland, where she became the country's first female monarch. In a further twist, she was crowned the King of Poland – a handy trick to get around the fact that there was no Polish tradition of royal succession through female kin.

After her father's death and her coronation, her marital arrangements were also thrown into chaos. It was decided that Jadwiga should wed Jogaila, the heathen ruler of

neighbouring Lithuania, so long as he vowed to give up his pagan ways and convert his country to Catholicism. William of Habsburg, however, refused to give up his betrothed – the pair had been promised to each other since William was eight and Jadwiga four. At one point, he even attempted to occupy Kraków's Wawel castle (the Polish kings' residence) to beg for her rightful hand in marriage. The lords of Poland, however, believed that the country would be better off if Jagwiga was married to Lithuania's king, rather than her childhood sweetheart.

If Jadwiga had any reservations about marrying Jogaila – there was an approximate 23-year age gap between them – she must have swallowed them, as she went ahead with the nuptial vows. Jogaila was baptized and took the Christian name Władysław, marrying Jadwiga shortly afterward. Perhaps Jadwiga realized that her own personal desire to marry a childhood friend had to take second place to the future of her new people. (Today, Jadwiga's act is seen in Poland as a symbol of self-sacrifice for one's nation.) William, for his part, always maintained that he was Jadwiga's rightful husband. He refused the compensation offer of 200,000 florins and did not take another woman as his bride until after Jadwiga's death.

Jadwiga and Jogaila ruled as joint sovereigns, with Jadwiga blossoming into a wise and powerful queen. She knew how to speak about five languages, and deployed these skills with great diplomatic finesse. The union of Poland and Lithuania was not uncontested – Jogaila's cousin Vytautus had launched his own claim to the throne in Lithuania and intended to seize the land for himself. Jadwiga nimbly defused the threat of civil war by negotiating a compromise between the two cousins, even paving the way for a long-lasting alliance between the pair.

But it was within her newly adopted country that Jadwiga truly won the respect and love of her people. Alongside other charitable works, she helped to resurrect the University of Kraków, which had been built by King Casimir III in 1364 and had fallen into disrepair; she even went to the extent of buying up the houses running along its nearby streets to expand its campus. Jadwiga died shortly after giving birth to her only child, Elizabeth, who survived for less than a month. Even in death, Jadwiga sought to provide for her people, decreeing that half of all her wealth should go to the university, and the other half be divided among the poor. It is thanks to this philanthropy, and her statesmanlike abilities, that she is considered "one of Poland's greatest rulers".[13] In 1997, the Roman Catholic Church canonized her as the saint of queens, and of a united Europe.

n 1991, public outrage followed a campaign launched by Spain's bishops to have **Isabella of Castile** (1451–1504) – or La Católica, as she became known – canonized as a saint. Roman Catholics, Jews and Muslims alike protested that the instigator of the Catholic Inquisition was undeserving of the Vatican's highest and most heavenly honour.[14] The anger was so heated that Pope John Paul II put a stop to the beatification process, though within a decade or so Spain and some South American bishops were fighting once more to get "Saint Isabel" recognized.[15]

The pitched battle over Isabella's legacy is hardly surprising. The woman who became Spain's first sovereign queen was many things: pious but bigoted, merciful yet ruthless, and wise but cruel. Over her 30-year rule, the two fractious kingdoms of Castile and Aragon became Spain – a world power that conquered most of Latin America and grew fat off its riches. But she also established and oversaw the unimaginable cruelty of the Spanish Inquisition, which tortured, executed and drove out many thousands of Jews and Muslims.

As the only daughter of Juan II and his second wife, Isabella was second in line to the throne after her older half-brother, Enrique IV. She was knocked down to third in line following the birth of her younger brother, Alfonso. Few expected that Isabella would ever rule, but Enrique was nicknamed Enrique the Impotent for a reason: he could not produce children.

One marriage annulment later, Enrique found success when his second wife gave birth to his first and only child, Juana. But dissident nobles believed that Juana was illegitimate and proclaimed Alfonso king instead. Unfortunately, Alfonso unexpectedly died in 1468 – and Isabel was once more second in line to the throne. Defying

Enrique's orders to marry the Portuguese king, she chose 17-year-old Ferdinand, the son of King Juan II of Aragon. The union would lay the foundations for one of the most fruitful royal partnerships in history. When Enrique died, 23-year-old Isabella declared herself queen of Castile – and when his father passed away, Ferdinand inherited the kingdom of Aragon.

Together, they began seeing off any threats to their authority. Ferdinand rode off to battle against Portugal to secure Castile's western border. Isabella, thrilled by the heat of battle, would ride out with army reinforcements to strengthen Ferdinand's troops. In the initial years of their reign, the two monarchs waged war against their enemies, launching a series of measures that snatched power back from the aristocracy and reclaimed it for the crown. Over a decade of intense conflict, they even conquered Granada, a southern kingdom that had become the only remaining bastion of Muslim power – thus wiping out the last trace of Muslim rule on the Iberian peninsula. Isabella was drawing up stratagems and leading negotiations even while pregnant – she was so deeply involved that she once went into labour during a war council.

The queen believed her foes lay not just outside Spain's borders but also within them. In 1480, she and Ferdinand set up the Holy Office of the Inquisition, a State- and Church-run tribunal that was chiefly tasked with ferreting out *conversos* (Jews who had abandoned their faith and converted to Christianity). Religious clerics had sworn to Isabella that these converts had not really abandoned their original faith but were "judaizing" in secret. Heresy was a crime against the State, and therefore a challenge to her own authority, so Isabella wasted no time in attempting to "purify" her country. Although she admitted to her Rome ambassador, "I have caused great calamities and depopulated towns, provinces and kingdoms," she maintained that it was only religious zeal that motivated her.

Within days, Inquisitors in Seville – the city that was home to the greatest number of *conversos* – had arrested some of the most wealthy and prominent converts and locked them up in jail. Respected priests, judges and monks were tortured, hauled on to a bonfire and set alight. Even the bodies of those suspected to have been secret Jews were dug up and incinerated. Given that people providing tip-offs were guaranteed anonymity – and the ensuing false confessions were all too easy to elicit under torture – the Inquisition became fuelled by a self-perpetuating cycle of lies and deceit. Eventually, Isabella and Ferdinand decided that the *conversos* were being influenced by the remaining Jews in Spain, and ordered them all to convert or face exile.

Ten years later, Isabella would exact the same price from the Muslims of Grenada. Many decided to leave their homes behind rather than give up their religion, and those who did convert quickly fell prey to the Inquisition. Isabella had succeeded in her aim of making Spain a Roman Catholic country – but at a hideous cost.

Spain was also prospering from the newly tapped resources of the New World. With great foresight, Isabella had lavished money, ships and men on Christopher Columbus's expeditions and other seafaring trips. Her explorers mapped thousands of miles of coast, reaching the Caribbean, North America, Venezuela and even the Amazon river. Spaniards signed up by the hundreds to seek these lands of unimaginable wealth, conquering every land they came across in the name of Isabella and Ferdinand. But here Isabella displayed surprising mercy, reacting with outrage when Columbus returned to Spain with a cargo of Native American slaves – she ordered them to be transported home and released.

By the time Isabella died in 1504, she had become more than just a usurper to the throne of Castile. She had grown into Europe's most powerful queen, responsible for spreading Catholicism – albeit through violence and colonization – through the world. She was the woman behind Coumbus's greatest discoveries, and the woman who assured Spain's emergence as an empire. As her personal tutor wrote to a friend, lamenting her death, "She has lived having surpassed every human height so that she cannot die; she will finish her mortality with death, not die."

ong before the countries of North and South Korea existed, the kingdom of Silla flourished as one of three kingdoms in Korea. With their antler-like crowns of magnificent gold and their abundant supplies of iron, the kings and queens of the Silla dynasty ruled over their people for eight centuries before it was conquered by a rival kingdom. It was, however, unique among the other dynasties that wrestled for control of the Korean peninsula: it was ruled by women three times. And none was more beloved or celebrated than Queen **Seondeok of Silla** (ruled AD 632–647), the first female ruler of Korea.

Seondeok came to power after her father, King Jinpyeong, died without leaving a male heir. Silla's bone rank system – a strict social hierarchy, in which family lineage was thought to be passed down through bone, not blood – meant that only those born to the Songgol ("Holy Bone") rank could become sovereign. The bone rank system governed all levels of society; your rank determined everything from your social status to the design of your saddle and the size of your home. When Jinpyeong passed away without a Songgol male to inherit the throne, the crown naturally passed to Seondeok. In this instance, it seems, bone trumped gender.

Seondeok was the first Silla queen to inherit power, but it wasn't surprising that women enjoyed high social standing in Silla. Political power was intimately tied to supernatural abilities, and Korean shamans were predominantly women.

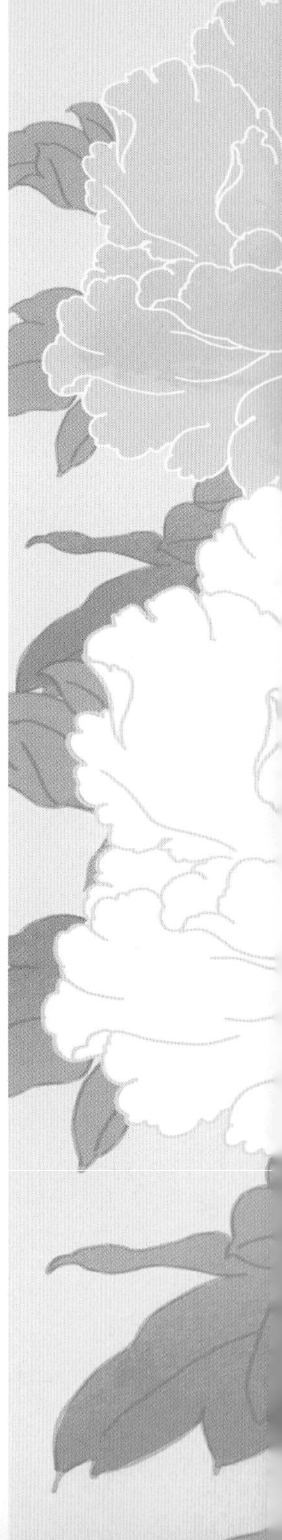

In fact, the most legendary accounts of Seondeok's wisdom are based on her skill of prophecy. In one tale, she correctly guessed that five hundred soldiers from an invading army were hiding in a valley west of the city – all because she had seen an unusual gathering of frogs in the Jade Gate Pond at Yeongmyosa Temple. "Angry frogs look like soldiers and a jade gate refers to a woman's genitals," she explained to her amazed courtiers, shortly after crushing the enemy army. "Female is *yin* and white is its symbolic colour, which also stands for the west."[16]

Though Silla was undoubtedly rich and prosperous, it was also under constant threat from the two other Korean kingdoms: Baekje and Goguryeo. The encroachment of these two states forced Seondeok to request military aid from China, Silla's trading partner and neighbour in the north. China's Tang emperor offered to send his army but suggested that Silla's troubles were down to the gender of its leader. The country would be much better served, he said, if a Chinese prince were to take over as interim ruler. Seondeok diplomatically turned down the proposal but still managed to cultivate an ally out of the powerful Tang dynasty, laying the foundations for a relationship that would later allow Seondeok's successors to triumph in the war between the three Korean kingdoms.

Technology and culture flourished under Seondeok's rule, with the grand capital of Gyeongju reaching ever greater heights with the construction of splendid pagodas, bronze bells and temples. Even today, the 9m (30ft) Cheomseongdae astronomical observatory, the oldest of its kind surviving in Asia, remains standing as a remarkable testament to the monarch who built it.

Seondeok adopted and encouraged the spread of Buddhism – then a fledgling religion that had wound its way from India through to China and Korea – as a way to enhance her own power and mystical authority. As monarch, Seondeok became regarded as an incarnation of the Buddha himself – a focal point of religious, moral and political authority. She was worshipped by her people accordingly. Another mythical tale regarding the empress states that a man called Jigwi was so full of love for Seondeok that, when she gave him a bracelet, his heart literally burst into flames and scorched the walls of a pagoda.

Sadly, many of Seondeok's greatest building works have been lost or destroyed with the passage of time: wooden pagodas, unfortunately, do not last for nearly as long as a gold crown. But perhaps the greatest measure of this Korean empress's success can be determined from her later descendants. After her death, she was succeeded by another woman – her cousin, Queen Jindeok – and, two and a half centuries later, by Queen Jinseong. Korea's run of three empresses would come to an abrupt end with the eventual demise of the kingdom of Silla – and, as historian Kyung Moon Hwang notes, Korea had to wait until the 21st century, with the election of South Korea's President Park Geun-hye, to be ruled by a woman again.

nown as the "first grandmother of Europe" and the "mother queen of the Middle Ages", **Eleanor of Aquitaine** (1122/24–1204) dramatically influenced medieval history through a combination of marriage, politicking and sheer force of will. Over the course of her lifetime, she wedded two kings and gave birth to three more, including Richard the Lionheart – and she outlived most of them to boot.

In her youth, Eleanor was the most sought-after beauty in Europe, thanks in part to being heiress of Aquitaine. With its abundant vineyards and fertile pastures, the duchy of Aquitaine was even richer than the kingdom of France. Eleanor was only in her early teens when she was married off to Louis VII in 1137. When he ascended the French throne, it was with Eleanor – and the wealth of Aquitaine – by his side.

By all accounts, Louis was besotted with his beautiful, sophisticated younger wife. But their marriage disintegrated after they set off for the Holy Land on the Second Crusade in 1147, which ended in disaster with Crusaders beset by starvation, Turkish soldiers and even plague.

Some believe that it was on this journey that Eleanor raised the thorny problem of consanguinity – the idea that they were too closely related by blood for marriage. There were also rumours that she began a torrid and incestuous love affair with her uncle Raymond, the sovereign prince of Antioch, though she was never formally charged with adultery.

Whatever happened on the Crusade caused an irreparable rift between Eleanor and Louis – a chasm that only deepened when, on their return, she gave birth to their second daughter and not the longed-for son. In 1152, Eleanor and Louis divorced, citing consanguinity as their reason. It was clear that there was no love lost between the two; two months after the annulment, Eleanor – then 28–30 years old – was married to the powerful Henry of Anjou, who was roughly a decade younger and would later be crowned King of England.

As king, Henry II was often away on lengthy military campaigns and his capable older queen acted as regent, administering his commands and working with his ministers. When they were together, they bickered and argued (though not enough to prevent Eleanor from giving birth to five sons and three daughters). As was traditional, Henry II crowned their eldest son, Henry the Young, as the new king and heir apparent while he was still alive – but still refused to relinquish his grip on power. As Henry II grew increasingly tyrannical and erratic – even ordering his knights to murder his former friend, Thomas Becket, Archbishop of Canterbury – his own wife and sons began to plot against him. Unfortunately, the Revolt of 1173–4 was discovered and summarily crushed, and Henry spared no mercy for his traitorous wife. Eleanor, then in her early fifties, was locked away in various castles for almost two decades. She was occasionally wheeled out when diplomatic necessity required it but was otherwise a prisoner of her own husband.

Almost anyone else would have crumbled in captivity; Eleanor merely bided her time, waiting for the moment that her captor died and her son, Richard, was crowned King of England. When this finally occurred in 1189, one of Richard's first acts was to

release his mother, whom he then appointed as regent. Richard was obsessed with making a success of the Third Crusade and spent only ten months in his own kingdom, leaving his mother to get on with the business of administration. Eleanor rode through England dispensing justice and doing business in her son's name, gaining the admiration and trust of her people. She even issued an amnesty for those who had been unjustly jailed, noting, wryly, "by her own experience that prisons were distasteful to men, and that to be released therefrom was a most delightful refreshment to the spirits".[17]

Richard's Crusade ended in failure; he did not reconquer Jerusalem and was even captured and held for ransom by the Holy Roman Emperor on the way back to England. It was Eleanor who raised the funds for his return and personally negotiated his release. She even engineered a reconciliation between Richard and his younger brother John, who had schemed against him with King Philip of France. On Richard's death in 1199, John became king, and Eleanor died five years later.

She was buried in a crypt in Anjou, France, between her second husband and Richard. After a lifetime of plotting, eternal rest must have come as some relief. Eleanor was queen of France, then queen of England, and governed the French duchy of Aquitaine for a staggering 67 years. She has been alternately described as an obscene seductress, a glorious patron of the arts and a conniving mother – even Shakespeare condemned her as a "monstrous injurer of heaven and heart". But thanks to her cunning and knack for survival, Eleanor triumphed over her enemies.

he history of the ancient world only occasionally references the presence of a powerful queen or regent, but rarer still are the female rulers who transcend the trappings of human flesh to become commemorated as gods. **Sammu-ramat** (*c.* 9th century BC), a queen who ruled Assyria centuries before the birth of Christ, is one of those.

Sammu-ramat reigned over the Assyrian Empire, governing a kingdom that sprawled across the vastness of Mesopotamia and stretched as far as Egypt. We must assume that she did not come to power easily – women were typically kept far away from authority in Assyria – but her rule brought a measure of stability and peace, of which the kingdom was in desperate need. Assyria had been torn apart and its royal coffers drained by sibling rebellion and civil war. The Assyrian prince Ashur-danin-pal was first in line for the throne but grew impatient, choosing instead to rebel against his father, King Shalmaneser III. His younger brother, Shamshi-Adad V, allied himself with the king and spent six long and financially draining years subduing the mutiny. When Sammu-ramat married Shamshi-Adad, the country was teetering on the brink of collapse.

Shamshi-Adad died before their son, Adad-Nirari III, was old enough to rule, catapulting Sammu-ramat into the position of queen regent of this monumental empire – which made her the most powerful woman in all of Mesopotamia, if not the world. The stela (a stone memorial slab) she had carved for herself is one of the few relics from her time, and it links her to the grand line of kings and monarchs that came before her – on it, she is described not only as Shamshi-Adad's queen but also, crucially, as Shalmaneser's daughter-in-law. Scholars believe that Sammu-ramat embarked on construction works throughout her kingdom and successfully quelled tribal rebellions in the north, securing the conflict-riven borders of the empire.

Little else is known about her reign. But Sammu-ramat clearly left a mark on her people – so much so that she was later transformed into a mythical goddess–queen. Some historians believe that the epic tales of Semiramis, an Assyrian ruler commemorated in Greek legend, are inspired by Sammu-ramat.

In one account by Greek historian Diodorus of Sicily, Semiramis is remembered as the love child of a common mortal and the Syrian fertility goddess Derceto. Abandoned by her parents, she is protected by a flock of doves, who keep her warm with their wings and feed her with milk, until nearby herdsmen discover her and adopt her. Semiramis' great beauty and intelligence charm first the governor of Syria and then his king, Ninus. In this

telling, she proves her military skill by coming up with an ingenious plan to invade the impregnable city of Bactra by scaling its acropolis walls, and in this way wins the heart of the king. (Her unfortunate first husband ends up hanging himself.) Semiramis inherits the crown when the king dies, and promptly builds an enormous burial mound in his honour – then embarks on relentless construction projects throughout her kingdom, including palaces, a ziggurat with statues cast from gold and other architectural wonders. She leads military campaigns in Egypt, Libya, Ethiopia and even as far away as India in a bid to expand her empire. Semiramis is both beautiful and ruthless; she takes lovers only from the most handsome of her soldiers, and has them executed the morning after. However, her life is cut short when her own son murders her. According to various incarnations of the legend, her body transforms into a dove and ascends to heaven or is borne on the wings of a flock of doves – the same ones that nurtured her as an infant.

It is difficult to say how much of Semiramis' legendary exploits were shared by the real-life Sammu-ramat. Certainly, it is possible that tales of Sammu-ramat grew larger and more fanciful with the retelling, until centuries later Greek historians and writers remember her more as a figure of myth than an actual person. But until more evidence of Sammu-ramat's reign is uncovered from the sands of Mesopotamia, folklore and legend are all we have by which to remember her.

The Activists

self-described "bitch on wheels",[1] **Sylvia Rivera** (1951–2002) was a teenage runaway who became one of the world's earliest and most passionate advocates for transgender rights. "In many ways," one writer noted in a *Village Voice* obituary following her death in 2002, "Sylvia was the Rosa Parks of the modern transgender movement, a term that was not even coined until two decades after Stonewall."

Growing up in North America in the 1950s and 1960s was brutal for young trans people, let alone a transgender orphan born into poverty. Her mother killed herself when Sylvia was just three and her biological father was already long gone. Sylvia's forbidding Venezuelan grandmother took her in but despised her love of makeup and would beat her if Sylvia came home with lovebites on her neck.

By the time she was ten, Sylvia was out of her grandmother's door and hustling with other street queens on New York's 42nd Street. These teenage hustlers were turning tricks out of financial necessity – most had been disowned by their families or found it impossible to get a 9–5 job in the prevailing atmosphere of homophobia and transphobia. It was here that Sylvia found her family, a marginalized community of outsiders that she would advocate for later on in life.

In the early hours of 28 June 1969, Sylvia headed to the Stonewall Inn in Greenwich Village to go dancing. She was about to turn 18. While Greenwich Village was a relatively tolerant and gay-friendly neighbourhood, the New York Police Department would regularly raid its bars to collect bribes, intimidate and arrest guests. By law, you had to wear at least three items of clothing deemed appropriate for your biological gender – meaning that trans women, butch lesbians and any other gender-nonconforming individuals could face a night in the cells.

That night, a police raid on the Stonewall Inn erupted into rioting. While reports differ on exactly what prompted the breakout of violence, Sylvia says she was right at the front as people began to throw loose change and coins at the police, shouting, "Here's your payoff, you pigs! Get out of our faces!"[2] As nickels and dimes turned into glass bottles, the police were barricaded inside the Stonewall Inn. At one point, Sylvia claimed to have hurled one of the first Molotov cocktails at the police.

"All of us were working for so many movements at that time. Everyone was involved with the women's movement, the peace movement, the civil rights movement. We were all radicals. I believe that's what brought it around," she later told *Workers World*. "You get tired of being just pushed around."

Sylvia was electrified; after years of harassment and discrimination, the LGBTQ community was finally waking up and expressing its rage. As the crowds swelled and began to fight back against the police reinforcements that had arrived, Sylvia howled through the streets, "The revolution is here!"[3]

After the Stonewall riots, Sylvia formed Street Transvestite Action Revolutionaries (STAR) with Marsha P Johnson, a trans black woman and street queen who had become her closest friend. At 213 East 2nd Street in New York, the pair created STAR House, a refuge where LGBTQ runaways like themselves could find food, shelter and clothing. Under Sylvia's direction, the organization would later go on to fight for key legislation such as the New York City

SYLVIA RIVERA
WAY

Transgender Rights Bill, which outlawed discrimination against trans people in housing and employment, and organized street actions to protest the murder of trans woman Amanda Milan in June 2000.

But Sylvia's wider participation in the LGBTQ movement was fraught with complications. She was deemed a troublemaker in gay organizations – a Puerto Rican–Venezuelan street queen who was too loud, too dark-skinned and too feminine to fit in with the white middle-class activists. Her concerns for those on the fringes of society – the trans street kids, queens and hustlers – did not endear her to most activists, who were focused on gaining mainstream acceptance. Others refused to accept her gender identity; at one rally, she was even denounced by lesbian women for "parodying womanhood"[4] and kept off the stage by people she had once called comrades.

As the mainstream gay rights movement fought hard-won battles for acceptance, Sylvia was there advocating for transgender people to take their rightful place beside them. A year before she died of complications arising from liver cancer, she was speaking at an event hosted by a group of gay male activists. She told them, with her characteristic aplomb, "*You* have acquired your liberation, your freedom, from that night. Myself, I've got shit, just like I had back then. But I still struggle, I still continue the struggle. I will struggle till the day I die and my main struggle right now is that my community will seek the rights that are justly ours."[5]

Lafayette Square lies directly north of the White House, a relatively modest-sized park with views to the entrance of the most photographed landmark in Washington, DC. It was here – directly facing the country's greatest seat of power – that **Concepción Picciotto** (1936–2016) called home for more than three decades. She demonstrated against the government through rain, sleet and snow, and her feat of endurance is thought to be the US's longest-running political protest.

With handwritten signs declaring "Read My Lips, No New Wars" and "Ban All Nuclear Weapons or Have a Nice Doomsday", her peace encampment became a well-photographed tourist attraction in its own right. From her vantage point, Concepción outlasted six presidents, observed countless dignitaries and diplomatic missions, and witnessed political dynasties rise and fall. This was all with one aim in mind: to be a constant reminder, to whoever passed through the halls of power, of the dangers posed by nuclear proliferation. Dressed in her trademark wig, helmet and head scarf, she became the White House's nearest – and most subversive – neighbour.

Concepción maintained a 24-hour vigil to swerve National Park Service regulations that prevent protest sites from being left unattended. Volunteers might step in to cover her if she left for some rest, but she was otherwise a constant presence through all four seasons. Like a political candidate running the longest campaign of her life, Concepción also tried to change the hearts and minds of those walking past, by handing out leaflets or speaking to tourists and DC locals about the importance of peace and nuclear disarmament.

EL PAIS

Concepción came to the US from Spain in 1960 and worked at the United Nations and the Spanish Embassy. But a disastrous marriage saw her husband run off with a mistress, along with Concepción's life savings and their daughter. In despair, she travelled to Washington, DC, to gain custody of her child. Instead, she ended up meeting William Thomas, an American trucker turned peace activist, who had begun a daily demonstration outside the White House. Concepción joined him in 1981 – and when Thomas died in 2009, she took over the vigil, which had already marked its 28th year of existence.

Not everyone agreed with Concepción's political views. In later years, her sidewalk sermons veered into diatribes against the Israeli government or took on a paranoid conspiracy-theory bent. Her trademark helmet, she explained, was meant to protect her from electromagnetic waves and government interference. Many simply wrote her off as crazy, though she fiercely denied any claim of mental health issues. Others defended her as a living embodiment of the First Amendment, which enshrines the freedom of speech and the right to peaceably assemble without interference.

That isn't to say that the peace vigil was welcomed with open arms by the White House. William and Concepción originally set up camp on the White House sidewalk, but were evicted by park police and the Secret Service. (They simply crossed Pennsylvania Avenue and set up camp in Lafayette Park.) Tents were banned, so she spent years sheltering from the elements under a white tarpaulin-covered umbrella.

Until volunteers stepped in to relieve the aging Concepción for occasional breaks, she even slept sitting up in a chair to avoid being moved on by anti-vagrancy laws that banned rough sleeping. And though she was never more than a short walk from the White House, not a single president strode over to say hello.

If Concepción was ever disappointed by this, she didn't let it show. Given that she dismissed all of them as corrupt stooges, she probably wasn't surprised by their unfriendliness. But she did live to see the immediate threat of nuclear war subside with the end of the Cold War, and Obama's pledge to create a world free of nuclear arms.

These advances may now have been thrown into doubt, but if there's one thing Concepción's 35-year vigil proves, it's that peace is a marathon, not a sprint.

"People always tell me, 'We need more people like you,'" Concepcion told the *Washington Post* in 2013, three years before her death. "I tell them: 'But it starts with you. You are responsible for what's going on.' If people were more concerned, I wouldn't have to be there."

n a chilly December day in 1999, the United Nations voted to designate 25 November as the International Day for the Elimination of Violence Against Women. Every year, countries all over the planet mark the date in a universal affirmation of women's right to lead a life unmarked by violence or harm. But few outside the Dominican Republic realize that 25 November commemorates **The Mirabal sisters**, three political activists who were assassinated on that day in 1960.

Patria (1924–1960), Minerva (1926–1960) and María Teresa (1935–1960) grew up in a country in the grip of a tyrannical dictator who had seized power in 1930: Rafael Trujillo, a military strongman who was as murderous as he was megalomaniacal. He slaughtered political opponents and killed thousands at the Dominican Republic's border with Haiti. He also garlanded himself with honours, nicknaming himself El Padre de la Patria Nueva ("Father of the New Nation") and even naming the capital city Ciudad Trujillo ("Trujillo City") after himself. And he was pretty much untouchable – he had amassed enormous personal wealth through corruption and had control of everything from the media to the army. In November 1960, he publicly declared that he had only two problems in his life: the Catholic Church and the Mirabal sisters.

Trujillo had good reason to be concerned. The Mirabal sisters were some of the strongest voices of resistance to his regime. The girls were born into a middle-class family in the El Cibao region of the Caribbean island, and were only young women when they had their first deeply unpleasant run-in with Trujillo.

Las Mariposas
Hermanas Mirabal

Infamous for his proclivity for young women, the despot would routinely send invitations to whichever woman caught his eye – requests that were never declined for fear of reprisal. The Mirabal family was invited to one such soirée, where Minerva apparently slapped Trujillo as he made his move. In retaliation, Trujillo ruined the Mirabal family – imprisoning the sisters' father (he died shortly after release), harassing the rest of the family and even barring Minerva from enrolling in university until she delivered a public speech praising him.

Given their father's fate, the Mirabal sisters might be forgiven if they had attempted to lie low for the rest of their lives. Instead, the 1959 Cuban Revolution lit the spark of sedition in them. At a small meeting among friends and political allies, María Teresa and Minerva argued that the Dominican Republic could follow in Cuba's footsteps and overthrow its dictator, like Castro had done with Fulgencio Batista. The Caribbean, they said, was ripe for revolution: "If in Cuba it has been possible to bring down the dictatorship, then in our country, with so many anti-Trujillo youth, we can do the same,"[6] Minerva reportedly declared. With Patria by their side, María Teresa and Minerva joined with other dissenters to form the 14th of June Movement, an anti-Trujillo underground network of rebels.

In 1960, the movement even came close to assassinating Trujillo at an agricultural fair – but the plot was rooted out by Trujillo's intelligence services. The Mirabal sisters and their husbands were rounded up and jailed, and a wave of mass arrests and torture ensued. Horrified, Trujillo's old allies began to desert him – the Catholic Church denounced him and the US turned cold. In an attempt to ward off international criticism, Trujillo released the Mirabal sisters but kept their husbands imprisoned. This was, however, only a temporary taste of freedom for the three women.

Trujillo had their husbands transferred to a remote prison accessible only via a road over a secluded mountain range. On 25 November 1960 – less than a month after Trujillo had made his public declaration on the problem posed by the sisters – the women were en route to visit their husbands when their vehicle was cut off by Trujillo's forces. Patria, Minerva and María Teresa were strangled and bludgeoned to death. Their bodies were dumped in their car, which was driven off the road to make it appear to be an accident.

News of their deaths spread through the Dominican Republic like wildfire, and catalyzed anger against Trujillo in a way that no other killing had before. This public outpouring of rage – once so unthinkable under his regime – marked the beginning of the end for Trujillo. Six months later, he was assassinated by members of his own military. The Mirabal sisters were transformed into national martyrs. Nicknamed Las Mariposas ("The Butterflies"), Patria, Minerva and María Teresa became three female icons of a revolution that took down one of the most brutal dictators of the 20th century.

n a Thursday in June 1956, **Lillian Ngoyi** (1911–1980) embarked on one of the most important days of her life. The South African anti-apartheid activist was about to lead twenty thousand women in a demonstration to protest the country's much hated pass laws, which required black African men to carry ID permits when outside their designated areas. Almost every woman had brought a petition carrying for the abolition of the unjust law, and the 45-year-old African National Congress (ANC) delegate intended to confront Prime Minister J G Strijdom at his office with this potent symbol of public disapproval.

But there was one problem – Strijdom didn't answer his door when she knocked. Instead, a voice from behind the door informed her that she was not allowed to be on the Union Buildings premises. "The women of Africa are outside," she replied. "They built this place and their husbands died for this."[7]

When there was still no response from Strijdom, Lillian left the petitions with his secretary and made her way to the thousands waiting outside. There, she did a most unusual thing – she commanded the crowd to fall silent for 30 minutes. Then, crying, "Strijdom is too much of a coward to meet with us,"[8] she led the women in a rendition of "Nkosi Sikelel' iAfrika" ("God Bless Africa"), a 19th-century hymn adopted as the official ANC anthem. That moment – when women of all races joined together in song – was a powerful expression of the anger and sorrow that ordinary South Africans felt toward the apartheid regime. It also bore Lillian's trademark inventiveness – never one to be put off by an obstacle in her path, she simply improvised around it.

Lillian was born in Pretoria in 1911. Working in a garment factory as a machinist, she signed up to the Garment Workers Union, a militant, non-racial trade union that frequently organized strikes. She quickly scaled its ranks to become an executive committee member, before joining the ANC, where her gift of public speaking did not go unnoticed. She was fiercely committted to the organization and was elected president of the ANC Women's League within less than a year.

AFRICAN NATIONAL CONGRESS
LILLIAN
NGOYI
ISITWALANDWE/SEAPARANKOE

"Mrs Ngoyi is a brilliant orator," a journalist from *Drum* magazine wrote in a profile of Lillian covering her "phenomenal" rise to fame. "She can toss the audience on her little finger, get men grunting with shame and a feeling of smallness and infuse everyone with renewed courage."[9]

Lillian's language was simple and unassuming, but she had a visceral understanding of the power of words. In a speech criticizing a proposed policy of segregated schooling, she cried, "My womb is shaken when they speak of Bantu Education... We women are like hens that lay eggs for someone to take away."

In 1954, she joined the steering committee of the Federation of South African Women (FEDSAW), the multi-racial women's group that would later organize the march on the Union Buildings. As one of its representatives, she even travelled illegally and in secret to speak about apartheid and women's emancipation in London and across Europe and Asia.

FEDSAW's goals were nothing less than the full emancipation of women of all ethnicities, including workplace protections, political representation and equal rights with men. The women's march would prove to be one of its greatest achievements, complete with a song and lyrics composed specifically for the movement: "You touch the women, you touch the rock. Strijdom, you will die!"[10]

Six months after the women's march, Lillian became the first and only woman elected to the ANC National Executive. That same month, she was one of 156 people – including Nelson Mandela – arrested and charged with high treason. Though all defendants were later acquitted, the four-year trial marked the beginning of Lillian's long entanglement with the law. She was arrested again during a state of emergency and thrown into prison, without trial, for five months, which she endured mostly in solitary confinement. In 1961, a banning order forbade her from travelling outside her Soweto neighbourhood, and she spent a further 71 days in solitary confinement after another arrest. She lived out the remainder of her life under banning orders that effectively turned her into a prisoner inside her own home.

But Lillian – now known as the "mother of black resistance"[11] – had not been forgotten, even after 11 years of confinement. When she died following an illness in 1980, more than two thousand mourners attended her Soweto funeral, and memorial services were held all over South Africa. When Nelson Mandela announced the ANC's electoral victory in the first South African elections, in which people of all races were able to vote, he paid tribute to Lilli, an, declaring her among "some of South Africa's greatest leaders... [who] should have been here to celebrate with us, for this is their achievement too".[12]

he British summer of 1976 saw London sizzling in 30°C (86°F) temperatures for weeks. As the UK baked in the heat, **Jayaben Desai** (1933–2010) – a diminutive 43-year-old factory employee – began her meteoric ascent as the leader of the "strikers in saris", the first workers' strike that saw South Asian migrant women link arms with white working-class trade unionists.

Jayaben was born in Gujarat, India, but moved to join her husband in Tanganyika, East Africa, where they enjoyed a comfortably middle-class life as one of the many South Asians who had chosen to settle in British territories abroad. But Jayaben and her family were soon forced to flee, after their adopted home country gained independence and embraced policies hostile to Asian migrants. Understandably, they leaped at the chance to resettle in the UK.

In fact, life at the heart of the British Empire wasn't easy. Jayaben's husband found work as an unskilled labourer, and she juggled childcare with a job as a seamstress. After bringing up their children, she took a job at Grunwick Film Processing Laboratories, a factory in northwest London best known for processing and developing holidaymakers' film rolls.

Jayaben was just one of the 440 workers who had found employment at Grunwick, many of them South Asian women. Newly arrived immigrants were often desperate for work, and managers at the factory considered them cheap, pliable and hardworking. But conditions at Grunwick were deplorable: Asian employees were routinely paid less than their white counterparts, compulsory overtime could be invoked without warning, and – most degradingly of all – they had to seek permission from their manager to use the bathroom. The managers operated out of a glass-walled room, from which they could observe everything happening in the factory. One protester describes a culture of "working out of fear".[13]

On a sweltering Monday in August, Jayaben led a walkout of 100 colleagues in protest at their inhumane treatment at Grunwick. As they left, one manager sniped that they looked more like a bunch of "chattering monkeys".[14] Jayaben replied, "What you are running is not a factory, it is a zoo. But in a zoo there are many types of animals. Some are monkeys who dance on your fingertips. Others are lions who can bite your head off. We are those lions, Mr Manager."[15]

Jayaben and the "strikers in saris" joined a white-collar union, APEX (Association of Professional, Executive, Clerical and Computer Staff), and started to issue demands for higher wages and better treatment. Grunwick refused to acknowledge the union and sacked anyone who joined the picket, which had then swelled to 137 people – well over a quarter of their staff.

Factory boss George Ward even came to the picket line to openly taunt the women. "One day he said, 'Mrs Desai, you can't win in a sari, I want to see you in a mini,'" Jayaben said. "I said, 'Mrs Gandhi wears a sari and she is ruling a vast country.'"[16]

To exert pressure on her former bosses, Jayaben began pulling every single string she could. The unionized postal workers at the local sorting office stopped handling post in and out of the factory, which meant that Grunwick couldn't receive any mail orders. The strike committee toured more than a thousand workplaces all across the UK to drum up support for the hundred or so women. Slowly but surely, the wider trade union movement fell in line behind Jayaben, and members were bussed in to protest alongside the original group of strikers.

By the summer of 1977, up to 20,000 people were picketing the factory, resulting in heated battles with police and mass arrests. On a single day in November that year, 113 people were taken into custody, and 243 protesters had to be treated for injuries.

Unfortunately, Jayaben was fighting a losing battle with Grunwick and George Ward, who refused to accept her union's demands. Eventually, her former allies in the Trades Union Congress (TUC) and APEX gave up on the fight. Jayaben and four other Grunwick workers went on hunger strike, but to no avail – their bosses would not budge, and the strike was dead in the water without the support of the TUC and APEX. As Jayaben bitterly observed later, "Trade union support is like honey on the elbow – you can smell it, you can feel it, but you cannot taste it."[17]

The two-year strike may have wound up in defeat, but thanks to the picketers, the workers who did remain at Grunwick got a better deal – including a pension. Most importantly, Jayaben and her strikers proved to their employers that immigrant women would not stand being pushed around or treated as less than equal to their white counterparts. "We have shown", Jayaben said, "that workers like us, new to these shores, will never accept being treated without dignity or respect."[18]

omen have served in revolutions the world over, but their contributions sometimes take shape far from the frontline, in medical wards and war hospitals. The act of tending to the wounded may not receive as much fame or glory as picking up a weapon, but it is vital nonetheless and requires just as much bravery. Nothing exemplifies this more than the life of **Nazaria Lagos** (1851–1945), the Filipino nurse and hospital director who is now known as the "Florence Nightingale of Panay".

When Nazaria was born, in 1851, the Philippines had been part of the Spanish Empire for well over three hundred years. But dissent found fertile ground in the colony's many islands, particularly on Panay, the fourth most populated island and site of Nazaria's birthplace in Dueñas, Iloilo. There, the Filipino people had resisted colonial authority for centuries; as far back as 1663, Panay locals had been killed by Spanish troops in a bloody uprising and their corpses mounted on stakes.

Nazaria was born an only child of a wealthy landowner; intelligent and gifted, she excelled at school. In keeping with tradition at the time, she was married off by the time she turned 12. Her husband, Segundo Lagos, came from a similarly illustrious family; his father had founded the town of Dueñas himself.

Since his apprenticeship at a local parish at the age of ten, Segundo had cultivated deep-rooted connections within the Catholic Church – an institution that wielded enormous power in colonial-era Panay. As an adult, he was made chief sacristan and entrusted with certain public duties, beginning with the 1897 construction of the first Red Cross in Iloilo.

FUERZAS
EXPEDITIONARIAS
DEL NORTE
DE
LUZON

As Segundo's wife, Nazaria had a comfortable, well-off lifestyle. She could speak and write Spanish fluently and mixed easily with the religious and political elite. Unsurprisingly, Segundo recommended her for the task of heading up the Red Cross. In 1898, Segundo left the Church to become the municipal president of Dueñas, as appointed by the colonial authorities.

However, the Spanish had no idea that their *presidente municipal* was plotting rebellion – and that his charming, well-educated wife was hosting revolutionary meetings with underground leaders at their isolated *hacienda* in the Borongan *barrio*.

With her Red Cross experience, Nazaria was charged with setting up a secret army hospital for rebel soldiers in the grounds of the Lagos estate. She was also appointed manager of the food supply for the revolutionary army – another important role for the forthcoming conflict. She moved into action immediately, transforming barns into food stores, growing plants for herbal medicine and directing the farm's *obreros* ("workers") to hack down bamboo and make beds for the newly converted hospital buildings. All the food, money and labour for the war effort came out of Nazaria's and Segundo's own pockets – they held nothing back.

When conflict came, it was bloody and protracted. In their war of independence, the people of Panay battled both Spain and the US. The end of the Spanish–American War in 1898 led to Spain ceding its old colony to the US, prompting the beginning of the Philippine–American War.

The US forces were brutal; if a village was suspected of harbouring rebels, soldiers would burn it to the ground, and civilians and Filipino soldiers were routinely tortured for information. This period of conflict was when Nazaria's field hospital saw the most use. As chief of the medical facility, she directed her medical staff and dealt with the wounded soldiers brought in by the bullock cartload. Nazaria worked tirelessly to administer to the sick and dying – she didn't quit even after a smallpox epidemic broke out and took the lives of two of her nine children.

Nazaria wasn't just the Florence Nightingale of Panay; she was also its Betsy Ross (who made the first American flag during that country's war of independence). In 1899, in the brief period between Spain's defeat and the US invasion, she helped to sew the Filipino flag that was hoisted in the centre of Dueñas. (One of the three gold stars on the flag represented Panay itself.)

But the war with the US would prove to be far more devastating than anyone realized. By the time Filipino forces had surrendered in 1902, Iloilo City was left a smouldering wreck, and Nazaria's hospital and some of the *hacienda* buildings had been burned to the ground. Nazaria was left to pick up the pieces of the Lagos estate as the Americans declared victory over the country for which she had sacrificed so much. But even though blindness claimed her sight in old age, she lived to be 93 years old and became an esteemed female icon of Filipino nationalism. Sadly she died in 1945, just one year before the United States granted independence to her beloved country, in 1946.

ary Ann McCracken (1770–1866) was only 28 when she accompanied her brother on his lonely walk to the gallows, taking his arm as he made his way to the noose. "I did not weep until then,"[19] she later said. At 5pm, Henry Joy McCracken was hanged on the land that their great-great-grandfather had gifted to Belfast, the city that Mary and her family had done so much to help improve. In the backdrop were four decaying human heads mounted on spikes – the remains of other men who, like Henry, had been convicted as republican rebels.[20]

In the face of this catastrophic loss, you might have expected Mary to withdraw from her Presbyterian family's many philanthropic causes. The McCrackens were well respected in Belfast – her uncle had co-founded the Belfast Charitable Society, which was responsible for building the Poor House (a shelter for the destitute) and the city's first hospital. While Henry's politics as a militant revolutionary for the Society of United Irishmen were not shared by the wider McCracken clan, both Mary and Henry were part of a long family tradition that sought to improve the lot of their fellow Irish.

But the death of her brother did not dampen Mary's enthusiasm as a social reformer. She would live to be 96, having straddled the 18th and 19th centuries, witnessing the profound upheavals that industrialization and the rise of republicanism brought to Ireland. By the time she was laid to rest in 1866, Mary had championed a dizzying variety of causes, including the welfare of children, reform of the prison system, and a halt to the dangerous practice of employing young boys as chimney sweeps. She had also raised funds for those too sick and poor to pay for health care, assisted victims of the Great Famine and, during her 19-year tenure as secretary of the ladies committee for the Poor House, improved the schooling of and welfare provision for the impoverished women who passed through its doors.

Mary's dedication to what was good and right extended to her personal life, too – Henry had a young illegitimate daughter, who had been left to fend for herself after his execution. Against the wishes of her family, Mary took the child into her own home and raised her herself.

But it was the rights of women and the abolition of slavery about which Mary felt most strongly. She and her sister Margaret had guaranteed themselves an unusual measure of financial independence by setting up a business that manufactured and sold embroidered muslin cloth. Mary dreamed of a future where women and men would experience true emancipation and be united in pursuit of the common good. She felt keenly the parallels between the horrors of slavery, the political oppression of the Irish under British rule and the domestic servitude of women – and saw her brother's republican cause as presenting the greatest hope of change.

"Is it not almost time, for the clouds of error and prejudice to disperse and that the female part of the Creation as well as the male should throw off the fetters with which they have been so long mentally bound?" she wrote to Henry before his death. "I think the reign of prejudice is nearly at an end, and that the truth and justice of our cause alone is sufficient to support it, as there can be no argument produced in favour of the slavery of women that has not been used in favour of general slavery."[21]

When Mary shut down her muslin business in 1815, she channelled her energies into becoming one of Belfast's most prominent activists. Her grand-niece, Anna McCleery, noted that Mary's strength of personality came out best when confronted with evidence of injustice: "She had naturally a quick and hasty temper, though evidence of this was rarely seen; but even when at an advanced age, if a helpless person were wronged, or an animal cruelly treated, it was startling to see how her eye would flash, and to hear her indignant words."[22]

Well into her old age, Mary never gave up on her beliefs. Even after Britain abolished slavery in 1833, she railed against its persistence overseas. When she was just 17 days shy of turning 89, she was distributing anti-slavery flyers to people setting out for the US, which she described as "the land of the tyrant and the slave". She even abstained from eating sugar to protest against its reliance on the slave trade. When she died, just before her 100th birthday, Belfast lost one of its greatest champions for the poor and marginalized – and as one tribute put it, "a life so rich in all good works, and a spirit so full of love".[24]

The Reformers

n the early part of the 20th century, one element was all the rage: radium. Thought to be a miracle cure for every ailment going, the newly discovered element was used in everything from lotions and toothpaste to drinking water. Even the US military had a use for it: radium made the clock faces of their soldiers' timepieces glow gently enough to be seen in the dark yet remain undetected by enemy troops.

Young women and teenage girls were employed in US Radium Corporation factories as dial painters, tasked with the delicate job of painting radium on the watches and clocks. They were instructed to wet the brushes in their mouths to make the finest point necessary for painting radium on with, a practice known as lip-pointing.

They were told by their employers that radium was safe, but nothing could have been farther from the truth. With every passing day in the factory and every dab of the brush in the mouth, they were ingesting a toxic substance. Radium may have lit their skin, hair and clothes with a beautiful, unearthly glow – but it was killing them from the inside.

In 1922, Amelia "Mollie" Maggia quit the factory. She'd worked there for four years, but now she was wasting away from a mysterious disease. One by one, she lost her teeth. Her jaw literally broke off into pieces. Her limbs ached with what was initially diagnosed as rheumatism. She eventually haemorrhaged to death.

Amelia wasn't the only dial painter who fell sick. Katherine Schaub's teeth fell out, and Grace Fryer had to wear a steel brace to support her back. Even after they stopped working at the factory, their bones fractured easily and their jaws crumbled; cancerous tumors sprouted on their bodies.

Five dying women – Katherine, Grace, Edna Bolz and Amelia's two sisters – tried to take US Radium to court. The press christened them **The Radium Girls**. It wasn't easy, though. Their former employers had no desire to admit wrongdoing, and the women struggled to find a lawyer to take their case. But Harrison Martland, a New Jersey medical examiner, and New York City toxicologist Alexander Gettler soon discovered that Amelia's exhumed remains were poisoned with radiation. It proved The Radium Girls were right – the radioactive element in their bodies was causing them to sicken and, in the case of 13 other women since the lawsuit had been filed, die.

By the time the Radium Girls saw US Radium in the courtroom, they, too, were dying. But they were motivated by other reasons. "It is not for myself I care," Grace declared. "I am thinking more of the hundreds of girls to whom this may serve as an example." After all, another dial-painting factory had just opened up in Illinois. Dozens more girls might be exposed to the same levels of radium that were killing them.

The Radium Girls sued the company for $250,000 each – a huge sum by today's standards. They won damages in 1938, but were given only months to live. Catherine Donohue, a worker in Illinois who sued her company Radium Dail, gave testimony while bedridden on a sofa.

Although these women ended up winning their cases, they faced resistance at every turn. Still, they refused to give up and eventually paved the way for what American workers now take for granted – that companies can be held legally responsible for the safety and health of their employees, and that people have the guaranteed right to work in a safe environment.

"Even nature seemed to have no place for me. I was neither a wee girl nor a tall one; neither a wild Indian nor a tame one,"[1] the Native American activist and author **Zitkála-Šá** (1876–1938) wrote in 1921, describing her childhood in South Dakota's Yankton reservation. She would battle this sense of alienation for all of her life and, in the process, would blaze a trail as one of her community's greatest voices for representation and change.

Born Gertrude Simmons to a Sioux mother and a white man, Zitkála-Šá ("Red Bird" in the Lakota language) began life in one of the most tumultuous years for conflict between Native American tribes and the US government. Three years earlier, gold had been discovered in the Black Hills, within the Great Sioux Reservation. Thousands of miners flooded into the region, in contravention of a US–Sioux treaty that guaranteed Native American ownership in perpetuity. War broke out when the US government mounted an aggressive military campaign to seize the land, claiming victory in 1877 after the surrender of a large majority of Sioux. Thanks to new laws passed in Congress, Sioux territory dwindled from 134 million acres to 15 million – and it was decreed that Native American children like Zitkála-Šá were to be extracted from their homes and educated in boarding schools to better assimilate into "paleface" society.

Zitkála-Šá was about eight when she was shipped east on the "iron horse"[2] (railway) to a Quaker school in Wabash, Indiana. She subsequently enrolled at Earlham College in Richmond, Indiana, against her mother's wishes, and discovered a knack for public speaking, going up against her white peers and winning oratory contests. She also studied piano and violin, playing violin for two years with the New England Conservatory of Music in Boston, Massachusetts.

But her assimilationist schooling was both a blessing and a curse; she would never fully belong in white society, and every educational achievement took her farther from the pastoral upbringing of her childhood.

In 1898, Zitkála-Šá took on a teaching post at Carlisle Indian Industrial School, in Pennsylvania. The school adopted an especially brutal interpretation of the word "assimilation" – students were beaten, deprived of food and even forced to labour for white families living near by. Discarding her English name in favour of a Lakota one, she began to publish autobiographical essays and short stories in *Atlantic Monthly* and *Harper's Bazaar* – writing that documented and celebrated Native American life and illuminated the cruel and distressing truth behind the education system. Knowing that her traditions were under attack, she also attempted to preserve cultural knowledge as best she could, through books such as *American Indian Stories* and an opera that re-created the Sioux Sun Dance – a ritual that had been banned by the US authorities.

Zitkála-Šá's causes were controversial at times, even among her own people. She campaigned against the use of the increasingly popular peyote, embarking on speaking tours across the Midwest in support of a ban on the "debilitating and degenerating"[3] ceremonial drug. She formed uncomfortable alliances with white conservatives who supported the anti-Native American policies that she passionately hated.

But Zitkála-Šá also became secretary–treasurer of the Society of American Indians (SAI), the first Native American-run advocacy organization, and became the editor of its accompanying publication *American Indian Magazine*. She blossomed into a passionate spokesperson and political campaigner for Native American rights, but expressed frustration at the glacial pace of change. "Everyone Indian who has attempted to do real uplift work for the tribes gets stung," she wrote in a letter to a friend. "No wonder that he quits trying, goes back to the blanket, and sits in the teepee like a boiled owl. I have not sense enough to stop. Wouldn't know until I was killed; and the chances are I wouldn't know then, being dead."[4]

The SAI was disbanded in 1919 after falling apart under the strain of internal dispute. Undeterred, Zitkála-Šá founded the National Council of American Indians seven years later and was elected president. Under her leadership, the group became a powerful advocate for Native American people. Guided by the official motto, "Help Indians help themselves in protecting their rights and properties", the organization grew to represent no fewer than 49 tribes. It fought countless battles with the US government for better legal and civic rights, spanning everything from improved ration distribution for reservations to land-settlement agreements and benefits for Native American war veterans.

One of her greatest achievements was an investigation into how oil corporations were defrauding – and even murdering – Native Americans in Oklahoma in order to seize their land. The resulting book, *Oklahoma's Poor Rich Indians: An Orgy of Graft and Exploitation of the Five Civilized Tribes – Legalized Robbery*, which she co-authored, prompted a government inquiry and led to the creation of what was called the "Indian New Deal" – a landmark piece of legislation that restored Native American land rights. Having fought all her life for the rights of her people, this tireless advocate died at the age of 61. She is buried next to her husband in Arlington National Cemetery, Virginia.

olitics isn't just about who gets to conquer countries, fight wars or make laws in government. It's also about the slow grind and struggle of those who work behind the scenes to make things happen. Nobody exemplifies this more than **Ruth Simpson** (1926–2008), a gay rights activist who toiled for decades to raise awareness of LGBTQ rights in the US.

In 1976, when Ruth wrote her pioneering book on lesbian identity, *From the Closet to the Courts*, gay men and women could be fired from their jobs, targeted by police or harassed on the street with full impunity. The majority of US states even legally barred gay people from certain jobs, including those in teaching, policing, law, medicine and even dentistry. If anything is testament to the work that LGBTQ activists like Ruth have done, it is that such measures seem ludicrous and unthinkable today.

But the world in which Ruth operated was a vastly different one. Born to two committed socialists deeply involved in the labour movement, Ruth was exposed to activism at an early age. By the time she was 12, her parents were taking her to picket lines, where she witnessed her father beaten up by a policeman. The result, however, was that Ruth disavowed politics – she had seen the heartbreak and anxiety stemming from her parents' activism. Instead, she studied drama and English at university and moved to New York to pursue a career on Broadway. But she found that she preferred being able to pay the rent, and therefore accepted a job at a PR company instead.

By the time Ruth went to her first Daughters of Bilitis (DOB) meetup in Manhattan, she was a high-powered executive working for one of the biggest public relations firms in the world. She had identified as a lesbian since the age of 16 but was afraid to come out of the closet. Her encounter with the DOB in autumn 1969 lit a fire in her.

"When I came to DOB, I saw the scars society had left on gay women, some of whom were filled with confusion, self-contempt, and fear," she said in an interview for the book *The Gay Crusaders*, first published in 1972. "And that's when I decided, 'You've got to move, you've got to start doing something!'"[5]

Initially founded in San Francisco as a secret sorority in 1955, the DOB was the first lesbian rights organization in the US; it had chapters in cities like New York, Chicago and Los Angeles. Ruth herself had felt little anxiety and insecurity about her own identity, which she said was down to her "truly remarkable, fabulous" parents[6] – but she could see the urgent necessity for an organization like the DOB to provide a safe place for marginalized women to come together. As she put it, "Lesbianism has a great deal more fiber in the tapestry – it's not just a matter of who you go to bed with. It's a whole set of mind. Just to pin it on sexuality is a great mistake."[7]

Ruth threw herself into DOB activity, becoming education director, acting president and then president in quick succession. Determined that the club would become a force for political change, she nurtured relationships with other LGBTQ groups to organize joint protests and demonstrations. She always trod carefully at work, but finally came out when the ABC network asked her to speak about lesbianism on a breakfast television show. One colleague told her never to speak to her again, but a senior vice-president of her company commended her on her dignified performance.

Under Ruth's guidance, the DOB began to search for premises to build a headquarters. Out of 75 places, they finally settled on a 370 square metre (4,000 square foot) loft in New York City's SoHo neighbourhood. Ruth supervised the renovations for what would become the first-ever lesbian community centre in the US, even building the wall framework herself. It opened in January 1971, with a colour scheme of red, black, yellow and white, to represent all the ethnicities of its members.

The centre was a roaring success. Hundreds of women attended its dances, and communal dinners heaved with donated food. As a more community-oriented alternative to a lesbian bar, it provided a place of support and respite from the overwhelming homophobia of the age. But it was also mercilessly targeted by police. Shortly after she became president, Ruth grew to believe that they had tapped both her home telephone and the DOB phone. In addition, officers would routinely burst into the centre without warrants. (Once, when Ruth asked what the members had done, an officer replied, "Oh, I think you know what you've done.")[8]

At one meeting, Ruth was threatened with arrest in front of 50 women, after a police raid found that the DOB didn't have a legally required occupancy sign. The charge was eventually dropped, but not before a policeman threatened to break Ruth's nose with his baton. It was the start of a long and sustained police campaign against the DOB. It made her even more resolved to fight for gay rights, but the more conservative members weren't happy rocking the boat. Eventually, internal divisions within the group forced her to resign.

Yet Ruth refused to be put off. She launched a career as a lecturer and began to speak on college campuses around America to raise awareness of LGBTQ rights. She wrote *From the Closet to the Courts* as a much needed antidote to the hysterical stereotyping about lesbians. At the age of 50, she moved to Woodstock in upstate New York and became involved in local politics, producing a weekly cable-TV talk show on politics called *Minority Report*. All through her life, she continued to urge all marginalized groups to unite and fight oppression – lesbians included. As she wrote wryly in her book, "Only when the person on the lowest rung of the ladder is free (this person is probably a black, poor, uneducated, lesbian woman who is left-handed), only when such a person is free can we all be free."[9]

hen **Shirley Chisholm** (1924–2005) ran for US president in 1972, she did so under one slogan: Unbought and Unbothered. At the start of her campaign, Shirley's student coordinator was tasked with picking up a shipment of brochures and bumper stickers from the airport. Somebody had graffitied "Go home, n*****" all over the box.[10] Shirley was not just the first woman in the race for the Democratic Party's presidential nominee; she was also its first-ever black candidate for the White House.

"I am not the candidate of black America, although I am black and proud," Shirley told voters in her native Brooklyn, in a speech announcing her intention to run. "I am not the candidate of the women's movement of this country, although I am a woman, and I am equally proud of that. I am the candidate of the people of America."

Shirley was no stranger to political firsts: in 1968, New Yorkers voted her in as the first African–American woman elected to Congress. "Just wait," she winked as she celebrated her victory, "there may be some fireworks."[11]

"Fireworks" turned out to be an accurate summary of Shirley's political career. Born as one of four sisters to Barbados immigrants, she impressed teachers and professors alike with her oratory skill. Her mother remembered three-year-old Shirley punching bigger children on the block and declaring, "Listen to me."[12] After getting a degree in elementary education at New York City's Columbia University, she became an educator and championed early schooling for children.

As a Congresswoman, Shirley never shied away from a fight. When she was appointed to the Committee on Agriculture, she demanded a different post that would be of more use to her city-dwelling constituents, pointing out, "Only nine

black people have been elected to Congress and those nine should be used as effectively as possible." Sticking up for herself worked – she was subsequently assigned to more important committees.

Shirley served in Congress for 14 years, but it was during her presidential run that she made her mark on society. According to Shirley, she stood to demolish the "ridiculous notion" that Americans would only vote for a white man. "I do not believe that in 1972, the great majority of Americans will continue to harbour such narrow and petty prejudice," she declared.

While on the campaign trail, she made a controversial visit to her political rival, Alabama governor George Wallace, while he was recovering in hospital after a failed assassination attempt. Wallace, with his extreme views on segregation and his racist campaign ads, stood for everything Shirley hated.

"Black people in my community crucified me," she told the *New York Times*[13] of the visit. But she believed that it was important to respect one's opponents, saying that to do otherwise would be to encourage "the same sickness in public life that leads to assassinations".[14] (Wallace, who is said to have wept all through Shirley's visit, was left paralyzed from the waist down and later renounced segregation.)

Shirley eventually came in seventh place among the nominees, and the Democratic Party selected George McGovern as their presidential choice. This didn't surprise her: she knew that she was not a favourite to win and that there was little chance that she would end up in the White House. Instead, Shirley's presidential campaign was a symbol of what had yet to be achieved – or, to put it more simply, she ran because she knew someone had to do it first.

It was a reflection of her conviction that politics ought to – and had to – be representative of the people under its power. "Our government, if [it] indeed is a democratic form of government, must be representative of the different segments of the American society," she said. "I feel that the cabinet and the department head of this country must have women, must have blacks, must have Indians, must have younger people, and not be completely and totally controlled constantly by white males."[15]

The symbolic campaign that Shirley undertook in 1972 would see its promise manifested in the Democratic primaries of 2008, when a young senator called Barack Obama faced off against Hillary Clinton for the presidential nomination. Four decades previously, it would have been unthinkable for a black man and a woman to be vying for presidency – let alone at the same time. But it had become possible, thanks in part to Shirley's efforts.

Before her death, Shirley was asked how she would like to be remembered. She had one request: "I'd like them to say that Shirley Chisholm had guts."[16] In 2015, when President Obama awarded her the Presidential Medal of Freedom posthumously, he paid tribute to her historic run – so instrumental to his own campaign – and confirmed, "I'm proud to say it: Shirley Chisholm had guts."

n a cold December day in 1941, **Jeannette Rankin** (1880–1973) ducked into a phone booth in a cloakroom of the Capitol Building of Congress and called for a police escort.[17] The phone booth was surrounded by a scrum of journalists and photographers,[18] all demanding to know one thing: why she had cast a vote against going to war with Japan. She had been the sole person to vote against taking military action. In doing so, she incensed fellow House Representatives and her constituents back in Montana. But if she had been disturbed by the booing and hissing she had received during the vote, she didn't let it show. Jeannette – already on her second Congressional run – was used to sticking to her guns.

Jeannette was born in Montana in 1880. Her mother was a New Hampshire-born teacher and her father a Canadian rancher. Her parents had moved to the frontier territory of Montana to seek adventure and fortune,

but Jeannette chafed against the strictures of her provincial hometown of Missoula, home to miners, cowboys and the 500km- (300 mile-) long Clark Fork river. After gaining a degree from Montana State University, she hopped between America's coasts, first as a social worker in a San Francisco settlement house, then as a student at the New York School of Philanthropy and subsequently at the University of Washington, Seattle, where she discovered women's suffrage and became active in the movement. "Go! Go! Go!" she urged in her diary. "It makes no difference where just so you go! Go! Go!"

In 1910, she witnessed voters in Washington state giving women the right to vote and took on a position as a lobbyist for the National American Woman Suffrage Association. By the time she returned to Montana, Jeannette was fully convinced of the suffragette cause. In a 1911 speech to the Montana legislature – the first ever delivered by a woman on its floor – she put forward a passionate argument for the vote: "We are asking for the same principle for which men gladly gave their lives in the revolutionary war. Taxation without representation is tyranny."[19] Three years later, Montana became one of six US states where women could finally participate in the political process.

Jeannette set her sights on the next challenge: becoming the first woman elected to the US Congress. She travelled thousands of miles in her home state, standing on street corners and knocking on doors to convince voters to take a chance on her, and they did: she was elected to the US House of Representatives in 1916. Her congressional debut made the headlines when, as one of her first acts as a Representative, she voted against going to war with Germany as World War I raged in Europe. She was pilloried in the newspapers, falsely accused of unseemly weeping in the House and scolded for setting back women's rights. Yet she would say later, "If you know a certain thing is right, you can't change it."[20]

That would be a sentiment she would hold dear for all her political career. Though her anti-war vote had infuriated other suffragettes, Jeannette worked hard to advance their shared cause. As part of the special committee on women's suffrage, she was instrumental in calling on the House to extend the vote to all women in the country. "How shall we answer their challenge, gentlemen," she declared to her fellow lawmakers, "how shall we explain to them the meaning of democracy if the same Congress that voted for war to make the world safe for democracy refuses to give this small measure of democracy to the women of our country?"

The amendment was defeated by the Senate, but was succeeded by the Nineteenth Amendment, making it illegal to deny any US citizen the vote; it was ratified and made into law in 1920. But Jeannette's pacifist stance drove away her constituents; she was voted out that same year, and began a second career as a peace activist and public speaker.

As the years wore on, Jeannette became increasingly concerned about the ever-escalating hostilities in Europe, which would eventually lead to World War II, and decided that there was only one thing for it. At the age of 60, she ran again for Congress. The electorate had forgiven her controversial vote; this time around, she comfortably won her seat, with 54 percent of the vote.

Then came a crisis: the Japanese had bombed Pearl Harbor, and President Franklin D Roosevelt needed the approval of Congress to go to war. This was when Jeannette cast her solitary vote, a single "no" against 388 in favour. It effectively ended her political career – she stood down at the end of her term and never sought to return to politics. But, in the process, she had stood firmly for her beliefs where others had capitulated, and she would become the only legislator to have voted against both world wars. To her, the choice was easy. As she would explain to friends, "I have nothing left but my integrity."

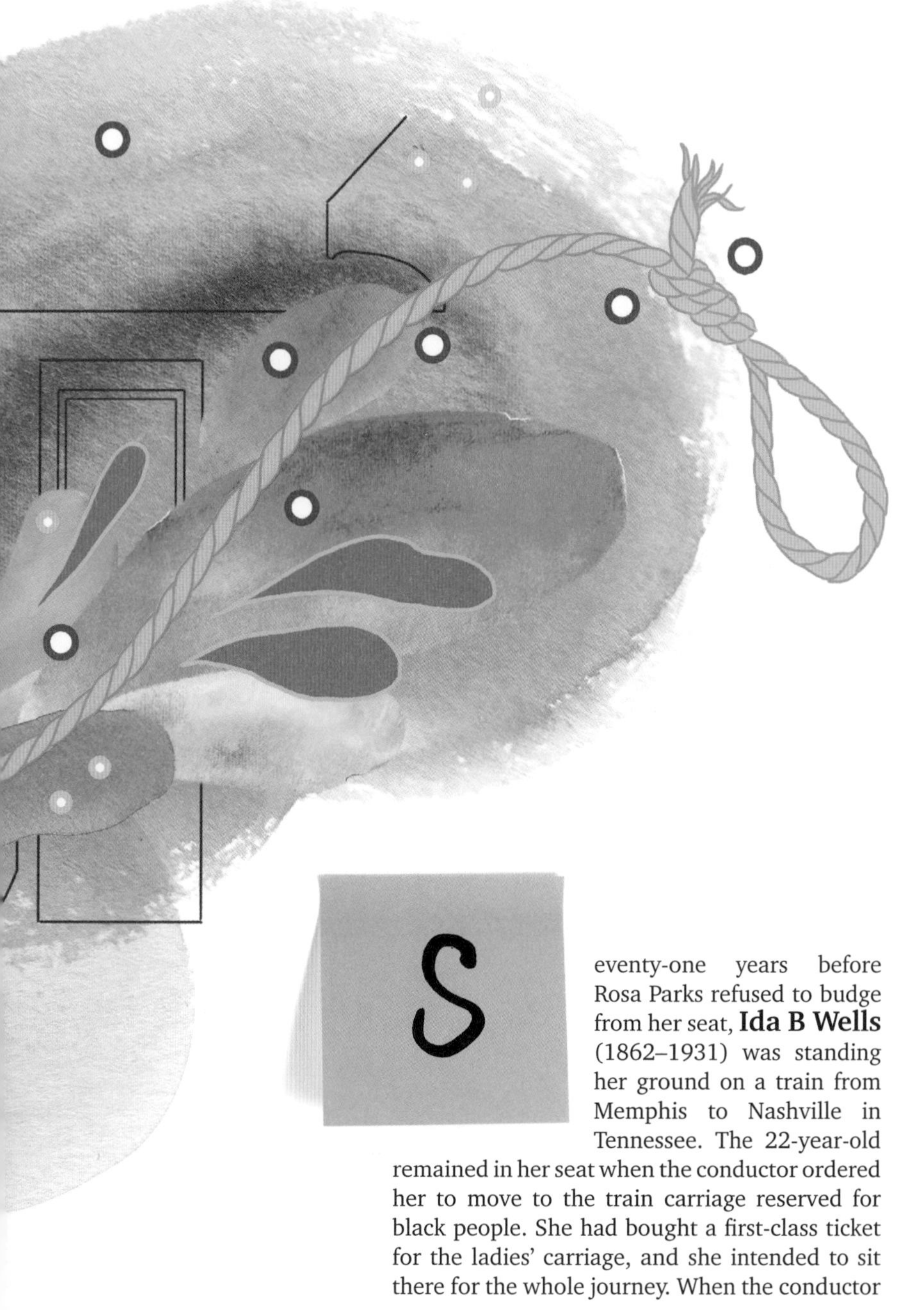

Seventy-one years before Rosa Parks refused to budge from her seat, **Ida B Wells** (1862–1931) was standing her ground on a train from Memphis to Nashville in Tennessee. The 22-year-old remained in her seat when the conductor ordered her to move to the train carriage reserved for black people. She had bought a first-class ticket for the ladies' carriage, and she intended to sit there for the whole journey. When the conductor tried to yank Ida from her seat, she bit his hand. In the end, three men dragged her out of her seat – so she sued the railway company and argued her case all the way to the Tennessee Supreme Court.

This would be considered bold in Rosa Parks's day, but it was even more remarkable in 1884. Ida had been born into slavery and was only five months old when the Emancipation Proclamation freed her parents from their slave owner in Holly Springs, Mississippi. She was part of the first generation of African-Americans to come of age as free men and women, and she would spend her entire life agitating for their long-awaited rights to be respected, embraced and fully realized.

At the time of the train incident, Ida was a teacher in Memphis, one of the more progressive cities in the South. Her outrage at her treatment on the train found an outlet when the editor of a weekly newspaper aimed at black audiences invited her to write about her experience. Under the pseudonym "Iola", Ida's sharply observed and incisive article instantly found an audience. But, although she won against the railway company, three years later the Tennessee Supreme Court decided to overturn her case. "I felt so disappointed because I had hoped such great things from my suit for my people," she wrote in her diary. "O God, is there no redress, no peace, no justice in this land for us?"[21]

Shaken but still undaunted, Ida continued writing, eventually editing and co-owning the *Memphis Free Speech and Headlight*, which she renamed the *Free Speech*. It quickly became one of the most radical and progressive voices for the black community in the city. In 1892, three black business owners – Calvin McDowell, Tom Moss and Will Stewart – were brutally lynched by a white mob. Appalled by the killings, Ida took to the editorial pages to denounce the violence and warn the black community that they were no longer safe in Memphis.

"There is therefore only one thing left to do," she wrote passionately, "save our money and leave a town which will neither protect our lives and property, nor give us a fair trial in the courts, but takes us out and murders us in cold blood when accused by white persons."

The *Free Speech* offices were ransacked and destroyed in retaliation; Ida was fortunate to have been out of town on business when it happened, but she received messages warning her in no uncertain terms that she would be beaten, dumped in the river or hanged.[22]

Ida settled in Chicago, where she continued investigating and exposing lynchings in the South. (Today, it is believed that up to 3,957 black people were murdered in Southern states between 1877 and 1950.[23]) She embarked on speaking tours up and down the country to raise awareness of the cruel treatment of African–Americans, and even travelled to the UK to drum up support for her cause. Ida firmly believed that the same barbarism and inequality that allowed slavery to thrive in the United States fuelled the epidemic of lynchings. "The lawlessness which has been here described is like unto that which prevailed under slavery," she told an audience in Boston. "The very same forces are at work now as then."

Her activism extended far beyond journalism. Ever alive to the intersections of class, gender and ethnicity, she campaigned for women's suffrage and founded the Negro Fellowship League in Chicago to assist migrants from the South and provide shelter for homeless black people. She was also a founding member of the National Association for the Advancement of Colored People (NAACP), which is now the biggest grassroots civil rights organization in the US. (Ida, however, never willing to compromise or back down, ended up leaving the group, as it was not militant enough for her.) Her passion even drove her to run for the Illinois State Senate, though she did not gain enough votes to get elected.

Ida died in 1931 at the age of 68, a passionate advocate for civil rights well into her old age. She did not live to see the passage of the Civil Rights Act of 1968, the landmark piece of legislation that ended segregation and outlawed employment discrimination based on race, colour, religion or gender. But if Ida had ever felt exhausted from her lifelong fight for equality, she never let it show. Even when she faced down threats to her life after the ransacking of the *Free Speech* offices, she dug her heels in, just as she had that fateful day on the train. "I felt that one had better die fighting against injustice," she observed, "than to die like a dog or a rat in a trap."[24]

n 1851, a middle-aged woman 1.8m (almost 6ft) tall, with a deep speaking voice and an unerring eye for a catchy phrase, got to her feet during the Women's Rights Convention in Akron, Ohio. "I could work as much and eat as much as a man – when I could get it – and bear the lash as well!" **Sojourner Truth** (*c.* 1797–1883) declared to the audience. "And ain't I a woman? I have borne 13 children, and seen most all sold off to slavery, and when I cried out with my mother's grief, none but Jesus heard me! And ain't I a woman?"

The "Ain't I a Woman" speech – which Sojourner delivered impromptu – went down in history as one of the most famous feminist and abolitionist speeches ever made. But there is much more to Sojourner's life than her most famous public address. Over the course of eight decades, this illiterate runaway slave-turned-reformer electrified audiences all across North America, penned her own memoirs and crusaded for social justice on issues like universal suffrage, the abolition of slavery and women's rights.

Sojourner was born into slavery as Isabella ("Belle") Baumfree, the granddaughter of an African man and woman who had survived the brutal Middle Passage (in which slaves were shipped under terrible conditions from Africa) to America, where they were sold to a rich Dutch family in a rural New York hamlet. When her parents' owner died, she was separated from her family and sold to a vicious English yeoman who had little reservation about stripping nine-year-old Belle and beating her until blood poured from her wounds. She was eventually sold two more times, finally ending up in the household of a landowner called John Dumont.

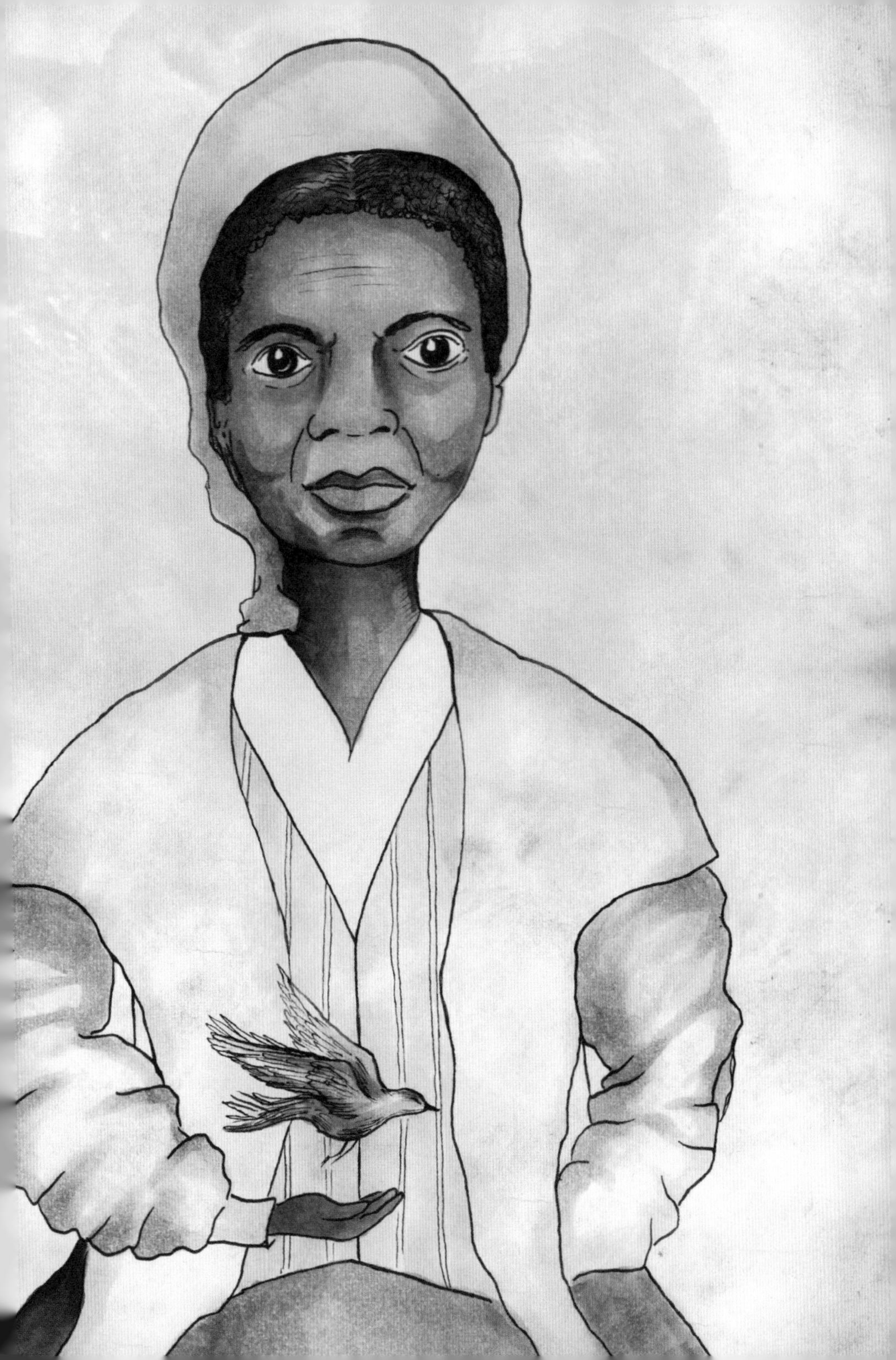

As Sojourner came of age in the Dumont household, New York was slowly changing in its attitude to slavery. In 1817, lawmakers in New York state promised that all slaves who were born before 1799 would be freed in a decade's time. But Sojourner's desire for freedom was growing faster than time allowed; she already had seen her mother die of palsy and her elderly father freeze to death after he was abandoned by his owners. Dumont promised to free her a year ahead of the emancipation deadline if she worked hard in the fields, and she began to labour with such intensity and determination that she accidentally chopped off a finger. Then Dumont changed his mind, claiming that the injury meant she had lost working time and so he could not free her ahead of schedule.

All her life, Sojourner had nurtured a deep sense of prophet-like connection to God, attributing her speaking talent to the divine and asserting that God's voice instructed her in all she did. Now divine guidance told Sojourner that she couldn't wait. Late in 1826, with a knapsack on her back and her daughter Sophia in her arms, she fled. A pro-emancipation Dutch family, the Van Wagenens, took in her and her child. They ended up negotiating with a furious Dumont to buy both Sojourner and Sophia for $25; in exchange, Sojourner would work off the money owed as a free woman.

Her first act of freedom was to track down her son, Peter, who had been kidnapped and sold by the Dumonts as a child. After a protracted year-long court battle, Peter was finally delivered into the arms of his mother. It was, Sojourner maintained, down to a higher power: "God only could have made such people hear me."

Life as a free woman was not always easy. Peter began dabbling in petty crime and eventually died as a seaman on a whaling ship, breaking his mother's heart in the process. Bereft of the son who she had fought so hard to retrieve, she turned to God once again: "Lord, whither shall I go?" she asked. A voice spoke to her, plain as day: "Go east." She obeyed, now reborn as Sojourner Truth. The Holy Spirit, she maintained, had ordered her to cast off her slave name.

She ended up in Massachusetts, at the Northampton Association of Education and Industry, a progressive Massachussetts commune that was founded on principles of spirituality, activism and equality, and where labour was split fairly between men and women. It was here that Sojourner began to develop her gift for preaching. After the community disbanded in 1846, she would spend the rest of her life speaking to audiences about the evils of gender inequality and slavery.

The crowds were not always welcoming, but Sojourner was more than equipped to defend herself. At one talk, a heckler voiced the persistent rumour that this powerful orator was a man in disguise. In response, Sojourner bared her breasts and told them that she had suckled "many a white babe to the exclusion of her own offspring…that it was not to her shame that she uncovered her breast before them, but to their shame".[25]

Her ability to silence, shame and charm a crowd earned her many admirers – a New York *Independent* journalist wrote, "I have never in my life seen anything like the magical influence that subdued the mobbish spirit of the day, and turned the jibes and sneers of an excited crowd into notes of respect and admiration." Through Sojourner, thousands of Americans were made aware of the evils of slavery and inequity – in 1864 she even met Abraham Lincoln and campaigned for freed slaves to receive land grants from the government.

But the true testament to Sojourner's abilities in persuading the nation perhaps lies in her final encounter with her former slavemaster. In 1849, she paid the aging Dumont a visit and found that he had renounced slavery. As she recounts in her memoirs, the man who had once owned her and her children – the man who had forced her to work so hard that she lost a finger – "said he could then see, that 'slavery was the wickedest thing in the world, the greatest curse the earth had ever felt'".

THE REBELS

1 Gott, Richard. *Cuba: A New History*, Yale University Press, 2005.
2 Ibid.
3 Chambers, Anne. *Granuaile: Grace O'Malley: Grace O'Malley – Ireland's Pirate Queen*, Gill & Macmillan Ltd, 2006. Page 2.
4 Murray, Theresa Denise. "Gráinne Mhaol, Pirate Queen of Connacht: Behind the Legend", *History Ireland* (2005): 16–20.www.historyireland.com/early-modern-history-1500-1700/grainne-mhaol-pirate-queen-of-connacht-behind-the-legend
5 Chambers, Anne. *Granuaile: Grace O'Malley: Grace O'Malley – Ireland's Pirate Queen*, Gill & Macmillan Ltd, 2006. Page 46.
6 Ibid. Page 62.
7 Compton, Mackenzie Faith. *The Sybil of the North: The Tale of Christina, Queen of Sweden*, Cassell, 1931.
8 Goldsmith, Margaret Leland. *Christina of Sweden: A Psychological Biography*, Doubleday, Doran & Co., 1935.
9 Ibid. Page 116.
10 Ibid. Page 73.
11 Ibid. Page 70.
12 Ibid. Page 205.
13 Ibid. Page 119.
14 Nelson, Cynthia. *Doria Shafik Egyptian Feminist: A Woman Apart*, American University in Cairo Press, 1996. Page 61.
15 Ibid. Page 74.
16 Ibid. Page 108.
17 Ibid. Page 121.
18 Ibid. Page 152.
19 Ibid. Page 62.
20 Lang, John. *Wanderings in India: And Other Sketches of Life in Hindostan*, Routledge, 1859. Page 95.
21 Versaikar, Vishnu Bhatt Godshe. *1857: The Real Story of the Great Uprising*, HarperCollins Publishers India. Kindle Edition.
22 Ibid.
23 Fraser, Antonia. *Warrior Queens: Boadicea's Chariot*, Weidenfield and Nicolson, 2002.
24 Gupta, Gautam. *1857 The Uprising*, Publications Division, Ministry of Information & Broadcasting, 2016.
25 National Women's History Museum. www.nwhm.org/education-resources/biography/biographies/355/
26 Kilmeade, Brian, and Don Yaeger. *George Washington's Secret Six: The Spy Ring that Saved the American Revolution*, Penguin, 2016. Page 54.
27 Ibid. Page 106.
28 Phaf-Rheinberger, Ineke. "Myths of Early Modernity: Historical and Contemporary Narratives on Brazil and Angola", *CR: The New Centennial Review*, vol. 7, no. 3, 2007. Pages 103–129. JSTOR, www.jstor.org/stable/41949567
29 Pearson, Judith L. *The Wolves at the Door: The True Story of America's Greatest Female Spy*, Diversion Books, 2014. Page 219.
30 Ibid. Page 216.
31 Ibid. Page 333.
32 Klein, Martin A. "Campbell, Gwyn – An Economic History of Imperial Madagascar, 1750–1895: The Rise and Fall of an Island Empire." *Histoire sociale/Social History* 39.78, 2006.
33 Berg, Gerald M. "Writing Ideology: Ranavalona, the Ancestral Bureaucrat." *History in Africa*, 22, 1995. Pages 73–92.
34 Ellis, William, and J J Freeman. *History of Madagascar. Comprising Also the Progress of the Christian Mission Established in 1818, and an Authentic Account of the Persecution and Recent Martyrdom of the Native Christians*, Fisher, Son & Co.,1838.
35 Pfeiffer, Ida. *The Last Travels of Ida Pfeiffer: Inclusive of a Visit to Madagascar, with a Biographical Memoir of the Author*, Harper & Brothers, 1861.
36 Skeie, Karina Hestad. *Building God's Kingdom: Norwegian Missionaries in Highland Madagascar 1866–1903* Vol. 42, Brill, 2012.
37 Kamhi, Alison. "Perceptions of Ranavalona I: A Malagasy Historic Figure as a Thematic Symbol of Malagasy Attitudes Toward History." Letter from the Editors-in-Chief, 2002. Page 29.
38 www.adb.anu.edu.au/biography/tarenorerer-13212
39 Ibid.
40 Boyce, James. *Van Diemen's Land: A History*, Black Inc., 2008. Page 319.

THE WARRIORS

1 Miksic, John N, and Geok Yian Goh. *Ancient Southeast Asia*, Taylor & Francis, 2016. Page 157.
2 Fraser, Antonia. *Warrior Queens: Boadicea's Chariot*, Weidenfield and Nicolson, 2002.
3 Taylor, Keith Weller. "The Trung Sisters in the Literature of Later

Centuries." *Southeast Asia: Past and Present*, ed. D R SarDesai, Westview Press, 2012.

4 Logan, William Stewart. *Hanoi: Biography of a City*, UNSW Press, 2000. Page 45.

5 Werner, Jayne, John K Whitmore and George Dutton, eds. *Sources of Vietnamese Tradition*, Columbia University Press, 2012. Page 56.

6 Pelley, Patricia M. *Postcolonial Vietnam: New Histories of the National Past*, Duke University Press, 2002. Page 179.

7 Ibid. Page 179.

8 www.britishmuseum.org/research/collection_online/collection_object_detailsa spx?objectId=327188&partId=1

9 Herodotus. *The History*, trans. George Rawlinson, Dutton & Co, 1862.

10 Ibid.

11 Ibid.

12 Ibid.

13 Ibid.

14 Ibid.

15 Heath, Jennifer. *The Scimitar and the Veil: Extraordinary Women of Islam*, Paulist Press, 2004. Page 216.

16 Heath, Jennifer. *The Scimitar and the veil: Extraordinary women of Islam*, Paulist Press, 2004. Page 216; Qazi, Farhana. "The Mujahidaat: Tracing the Early Female Warriors of Islam", *Women, Gender and Terrorism* (2011). Page 34.

17 Heath, Jennifer. *The Scimitar and the veil: Extraordinary women of Islam*, Paulist Press, 2004. Page 216.

18 Cummins, Antony. *In Search of the Ninja: The Historical Truth of Ninjutsu*, The History Press, 2012.

19 Ibid. Page 224.

20 Yan, Haiping. *Chinese Women Writers and the Feminist Imagination, 1905–1948*, Routledge, 2006. Page 43.

21 Edwards, Louise P. Gender, *Politics, and Democracy: Women's Suffrage in China*, Stanford University Press, 2008. Page 61.

22 Ibid.

23 Wang, Zheng. *Women in the Chinese Enlightenment: Oral and Textual Histories*, University of California Press, 1999. Page 43.

24 Fan, Hong. *Footbinding, Feminism, and Freedom: The Liberation of Women's Bodies in Modern China*, Vol. 1, Psychology Press, 1997. Page 91.

25 Ibid.

26 Edwards, Louise. *Women Warriors and Wartime Spies of China*, Cambridge University Press, 2016. Page 47.

27 Edwards, Louise P. *Gender, Politics, and Democracy: Women's Suffrage in China*, Stanford University Press, 2008. Page 62.

28 Finnane, Antonia. *Changing Clothes in China: Fashion, History, Nation*, Columbia University Press, 2008. Page 91.

29 Edwards, Louise. *Women Warriors and Wartime Spies of China*, Cambridge University Press, 2016. Page 48.

30 Williams, Jean. *A Contemporary History of Women's Sport, Part One: Sporting Women, 1850–1960*, Vol. 3. Routledge, 2014. Page 84.

31 www.ejmas.com/jnc/jncart_garrud_1299.htm#FN2

32 Godfrey, Emelyne. *Femininity, Crime and Self-Defence in Victorian Literature and Society: From Dagger-Fans to Suffragettes*, Springer, 2012. Page 101.

33 Ibid.

34 Wolf, Tony, and Kathrynne Wolf (ed). *Edith Garrud: The Suffragette Who Knew Jujutsu*, Lulu Press Inc, 2013. Page 78.

35 Winsbury, Rex. *Zenobia of Palmyra: History, Myth and the Neo-classical Imagination*, Duckworth, 2010.

36 Stoneman, Richard. *Palmyra and its Empire: Zenobia's Revolt against Rome*, University of Michigan Press, 1994.

37 Ibid.

38 Ibid. Page 175.

39 Ibid. Page 175.

40 Amadiume, Ifí. "African Women: Voicing Feminisms and Democratic Futures." *International Feminisms: Divergent Perspectives*, Vol. 10. Spring 2001. Page 55.

41 Madden, Annette. *In Her Footsteps: 101 Remarkable Black Women from the Queen of Sheba to Queen Latifah*, Conari Press, 2000. Page 8.

42 Fraser, Antonia. *Warrior Queens: Boadicea's Chariot*, Weidenfield and Nicolson, 2002.

43 De Pauw, Linda Grant. *Battle Cries and Lullabies: Women in War from Prehistory to the Present*, University of Oklahoma Press, 2014. Page 102.

44 Fraser, Antonia. *Warrior Queens: Boadicea's Chariot*, Weidenfield and Nicolson, 2002

45 Ibid.

46 Hay, David J. *The Military Leadership of Matilda of Canossa, 1046–1115*, Manchester University Press, 2008. Page 204.

47 Ibid.

48 Eastmond, Antony. "Gender and Orientalism in Georgia in the Age of Queen Tamar", *Women, Men and Eunuchs: Gender in Byzantium*, ed. Liz James, Routledge, 1997. Page 100.

49 Fraser, Antonia. *Warrior Queens: Boadicea's Chariot*, Weidenfield and Nicolson, 2002.

50 Ibid.

51 Monter, William. *The Rise of Female Kings in Europe, 1300–1800*, Yale University

Press, 2012. Page 12.
52 Fraser, Antonia. *Warrior Queens: Boadicea's Chariot*, Weidenfield and Nicolson, 2002.
53 Eastmond, Antony. "Gender and Orientalism in Georgia in the Age of Queen Tamar", *Women, Men and Eunuchs: Gender in Byzantium*, ed. Liz James, Routledge, 1997. Page 100.

THE RULERS

1 Fletcher, J. *The Story of Egypt*, Hodder, 2016. Page 207.
2 Weatherford, Jack. *The Secret History of the Mongol Queens: How the Daughters of Genghis Khan Rescued his Empire*, Broadway Books, 2011. Page 54.
3 Weatherford, Jack. *Genghis Khan and the Making of the Modern World*, Broadway Books, 2004.
4 Weatherford, Jack. *The Secret History of the Mongol Queens: How the Daughters of Genghis Khan Rescued his Empire*, Broadway Books, 2011. Page 115.
5 Gregory of Tours, *History of the Franks*, trans. Ernest Brehaut (extended selections), Records of Civilization 2, Columbia University Press, 1916.
6 Fredegar, Fredegarii *Chronicorum Liber Quartus cum Continuationibus*, trans. J M Wallace Hadrill, 4.17, 1960.
7 Garland, Lynda. *Byzantine Empresses: Women and Power in Byzantium AD 527–1204*. Routledge, 2002. Page 143.
8 Connor, Carolyn L. *Women of Byzantium*. Yale University Press, 2004. Page 235.
9 Frieda, Leonie. *Catherine de Medici: A Biography*, Hachette UK, 2011.
10 Accilien, Cécile, "Anacoana, the Golden Flower" in Accilien, Cécile, Jessica Adams, and Elmide Méléance ed. *Revolutionary Freedoms: A History of Survival, Strength and Imagination in Haiti*, Educa Vision Inc., 2006. Page 75.
11 Kizevetter, Aleksandr A. "Portrait of an Enlightened Autocrat." *Catherine the Great*, Palgrave Macmillan UK, 1972. Pages 3–20.
12 Massie, Robert K. *Catherine the Great: Portrait of a Woman*, Random House Inc., 2011. Pages 117–20.
13 Gromada, Thaddeus V. "Oscar Halecki's Vision of Saint Jadwiga of Anjou." *The Polish Review*, vol. 44, no. 4, 1999. Pages 433–7. JSTOR, www.jstor.org/stable/25779153
14 www.nytimes.com/1991/04/06/opinion/isabella-is-no-saint.html
15 www.theguardian.com/world/2002/mar/04internationaleducationnews.humanities
16 Lee, Bae-Yong. *Women in Korean History*, Ewha Womans University Press, 2008. Page 138.
17 Weir, Alison. *Eleanor of Aquitaine: By the Wrath of God, Queen of England*, Random House, 2008. Page 281.

THE ACTIVISTS

1 Bronski, Michael. "Sylvia Rivera: 1951–2002", *Z Magazine*, 1 April, 2012.
2 Rivera, Sylvia. "Sylvia Rivera's Talk at LGMNY, June 2001 Lesbian and Gay Community Services Center, New York City." *Centro Journal*, 19.1, 2007.
3 Ibid.
4 Gan, Jessi. "Still at the Back of the Bus: Sylvia Rivera's Struggle", *CENTRO: Journal of the Center for Puerto Rican Studies*, 19.1, 2007. Pages 124–140.
5 Rivera, Sylvia. "Sylvia Rivera's Talk at LGMNY, June 2001 Lesbian and Gay Community Services Center, New York City", *Centro Journal*, 19.1, 2007.
6 Robinson, Nancy. "Women's Political Participation in the Dominican Republic: The Case of the Mirabal Sisters", *Caribbean Quarterly*, vol. 52, no. 2/3, 2006. Pages 172–83. JSTOR, www.jstor.org/stable/40654568
7 Gasa, Nomboniso, ed. *Women in South African History: They Remove Boulders and Cross Rivers*, HSRC Press, 2007. Page 222.
8 Ibid. Page 223.
9 Ibid. Page 196.
10 Ibid. Page 223.
11 www.encyclopedia.com/history/encyclopedias-almanacs-transcripts-and-maps/lillian-ngoyi
12 www.mandela.gov.za/mandela_speeches/1994/940502_anc.htm
13 www.striking-women.org/module/striking-out/grunwick-dispute
14 www.bbc.co.uk/news/uk-england-london-37244466
15 www.theguardian.com/politics/2010/dec/28/jayaben-desai-obituary
16 Centre for Contemporary Cultural Studies, University of Birmingham. *The Empire Strikes Back: Race and Racism in 70s Britain*, Hutchinson, 1982. Page 260.
17 www.striking-women.org/module/striking-out/grunwick-dispute
18 www.bbc.co.uk/news/magazine-12110810
19 "McCracken, Mary Ann (1770–1866)", *Women in World History: A Biographical Encyclopedia*. www.encyclopedia.com/women/encyclopedias-almanacs-transcripts-and-maps/mccracken-mary-ann-1770-1866
20 www.belfasttelegraph.co.uk/imported/united-irish-rebel-hanged-28351243.html

21 "McCracken, Mary Ann (1770–1866)", *Women in World History: A Biographical Encyclopedia.* www.encyclopedia.com/women/encyclopedias-almanacs-transcripts-and-maps/mccracken-mary-ann-1770-1866
22 Ibid.
23 Ibid.
24 Ibid.

THE REFORMERS

1 Zitkála-Šá (aka Gertrude Simmons Bonnin). *American Indian Stories*, Hayworth Publishing House, 1921.
2 Ibid.
3 Davidson, Cathy N., and Ada Norris, eds. *American Indian Stories, Legends, and Other Writings*, Penguin, 2003.
4 Lewandowski, Tadeusz. *Red Bird, Red Power: The Life and Legacy of Zitkála-Šá,* Vol. 67, University of Oklahoma Press, 2016.
5 Tobin, Kay. *Gay Crusaders*, Arnu Press, 1975. Page 157.
6 ibid. Page 159.
7 ibid. Page 159.
8 Simpson, Ruth. *From the Closet to the Courts*, Penguin, 1977. Page 124.
9 ibid. Page 168.
10 www.smithsonianmag.com/smithsonian-institution/when-shirley-chisholm-ran-for-president-few-would-say-im-with-her-180958699/
11 www.nytimes.com/2005/01/03/obituaries/shirley-chisholm-unbossedpioneer-in-congress-is-dead-at-80.html?module=ArrowsNav&contentCollection=Obituaries&action=keypress®ion=FixedLeft&pgtype=article
12 Ibid.
13 www.nytimes.com/2005/01/03/obituaries/shirley-chisholm-unbossedpioneer-in-congress-is-dead-at-80.html?module=ArrowsNav&contentCollection=Obituaries&action=keypress®ion=FixedLeft&pgtype=article
14 www.theatlantic.com/magazine/archive/2016/10/the-radical-and-the-racist/497510/
15 www.pbs.org/newshour/rundown/what-former-presidential-candidate-shirley-chisholm-said-about-facing-gender-discrimination/
16 www.nytimes.com/2005/01/03/obituaries/shirley-chisholm-unbossedpioneer-in-congress-is-dead-at-80.html?module=ArrowsNav&contentCollection=Obituaries&action=keypress®ion=FixedLeft&pgtype=article
17 www.visitthecapitol.gov/exhibitions/timeline/image/capitol-phone-booth-jeannette-rankin-calls-assistance-following-her-vote
18 www.gettyimages.co.uklicense/515617134
19 www.montanaheritageproject.org/edheritage/1910/pridocs/1911rankin.htm
20 O'Brien, M B. *Jeannette Rankin: Bright Star in the Big Sky*, Twodot Books, 2015. Page 50.
21 Wells, Ida B. *Crusade for Justice: The Autobiography of Ida B Wells*, University of Chicago Press, 2013.
22 www.antislavery.eserver.org/legacies/lynch-law-in-all-its-phases/lynch-law-in-all-its-phases.pdf
23 www.washingtonpost.com/news/post-nation/wp/2015/02/10/even-more-black-people-were-lynched-in-the-u-s-than-previously-thought-study-finds/?utm_term=.d8dbf26f72b0
24 McMurry, Linda O. *To Keep the Waters Troubled: The Life of Ida B Wells*, Oxford University Press on Demand, 2000. Page 149.
25 Truth, Sojourner. *A Life, A Symbol*, W W Norton & Co., 1996. Pages 229–32.

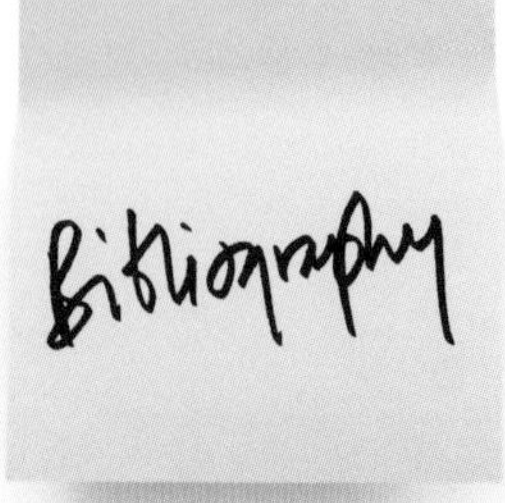

THE REBELS

Carlotta Lucumí (unknown–1844)
Araujo, Ana Lucia. *Shadows of the slave past: memory, heritage, and slavery*, Routledge, 2014
Campbell, Joan-Yvette. *In Search of Respect and Equality: Life Incidents of Slave and Free Women in North America and European Colonies*, Create Space, 2012
Finch, Aisha. "'What Looks Like a Revolution': Enslaved Women and the Gendered Terrain of Slave Insurgencies in Cuba, 1843–1844". *Journal of Women's History* 26.1 (2014): 112-134
Godfried, Eugene. 'Carlota', *AfroCubaWeb*, www.afrocubaweb.com/Carlota.htm
Gott, Richard. Cuba: *A new history*, Yale University Press, 2005
Houser, Myra Ann. "Avenging Carlota in Africa: Angola and the memory of Cuban slavery". *Atlantic Studies* 12.1, 2015, 50–66
Murray, David R. "Statistics of the slave trade to Cuba, 1790–1867". *Journal of Latin American Studies* 3.2, 1971, 131–49

Grace O'Malley (1530–1603)
Chambers, Anne. *Granuaile: Grace O'Malley: Grace O'Malley-Ireland's Pirate Queen*, Gill & Macmillan Ltd, 2006
Cook, Judith. *Pirate Queen: The Life of Grace O'Malley, 1530-1603*, Mercier Press Ltd, 2004
Murray, Theresa Denise. "Gráinne Mhaol, Pirate Queen of Connacht: Behind the Legend". *History Ireland*, 2005, 16–20

Christina of Sweden (1626–1689)
Buckley, Veronica. *Christina Queen of Sweden: The Restless Life of a European Eccentric*, HarperCollins UK, 2011
Compton, Mackenzie Faith. *The Sybil of the North: The Tale of Christina, Queen of Sweden*, Cassell, 1931
Goldsmith, Margaret Leland. *Christina of Sweden: a psychological biography*, Doubleday, Doran & Company, 1935
Waters, Sarah. "'A Girton Girl on a Throne': Queen Christina and Versions of Lesbianism, 1906-1933". *Feminist Review* 46, 1994, 41–60

Doria Shafik (1908–1975)
Nelson, Cynthia. *Doria Shafik Egyptian Feminist: A Woman Apart*, American University in Cairo Press, 1996
Nelson, Cynthia, et al. "Doria Shafik's French Writing: Hybridity in a Feminist Key", *Alif: Journal of Comparative Poetics*, no. 20, 2000, 109–39, www.jstor.org/stable/521944
Zuhur, Sherifa. "Doria Shafik, Egyptian Feminist: A Woman Apart", *Middle East Studies Association Bulletin* Vol.31, No.2, December 1997, 194–6, www.jstor.org/stable/23061460
www.doria-shafik.com/womens-rights-egypt-feminism-middle-east-13.html. Accessed 17 May, 2017

Lakshmibai (1828–1858)
Fraser, Antonia. *Warrior Queens: Boadicea's Chariot*, Weidenfield and Nicolson, 2002
Gupta, Gautam. *1857 THE UPRISING*, Publications Division Ministry of Information & Broadcasting, 2016
Versaikar, Vishnu Bhatt Godshe. *1857: The Real Story Of The Great Uprising*, HarperCollins Publishers India, 2011
www.atlasobscura.com/articles/lakshmibai-the-warrior-queen-who-fought-british-rule-in-india. Accessed 14 May, 2017
www.copsey-family.org/~allenc/lakshmibai/index.html. Accessed14 May, 2017

Agent 355 (dates unknown)
Kilmeade, Brian, and Don Yaeger. *George Washington's Secret Six: The Spy Ring that Saved the American Revolution*, Penguin, 2016
www.web.archive.org/web/20161108020943/https://www.nwhm.org/education-resources/biography/biographies/355/. Accessed 17 May, 2017

Noor Inayat Khan (1914–1944)
Basu, Shrabani, and M. R. D. Foot. *Spy Princess: The Life of Noor Inayat Khan*, The History Press, 2011
Basu, Shrabani, "The Sufi Spy who Saved Europe", *Newsweek*, 6 April 2014
Dalton, Samantha, "Noor Inayat Khan: The Indian princess who spied for Britain', *BBC News*, www.bbc.co.uk/news/uk-20240693. Accessed 24 January, 2017
Khadim, Tanveer, "Noor Inayat Khan: The Muslim WWII heroine who helped Jews", *The Express Tribune Blogs*, www.blogs.tribune.com.pk/story/24058/noor-inayat-khan-the-muslim-wwii-heroine-who-helped-jews/. Accessed 24 January, 2017
Tonkin, Boyd. "Noor Anayat Khan: The princess who became a spy", *Independent*, 20 February 2006
www.npr.org/2014/09/06/346049148/one-woman-many-surprises-pacifist-muslim-british-spy-wwii-hero. Accessed 24 January, 2017

Njinga Mbandi (1581/2–1663)
Banerji, Urvija. "Portuguese Slave Traders Were No Match for Angolan Queen Nzinga Mbandi", *Atlas Obscura*, www.atlasobscura.com/articles/portuguese-slave-traders-were-no-match-for-angolan-queen-nzinga-mbandi. Accessed 21 May, 2017
Heywood, Linda M. *Njinga of Angola: Africa's Warrior Queen*, Harvard University Press, 2017
Jackson, Guida M. *Women Leaders of Africa, Asia, Middle East, and Pacific: A Biographical Reference*, Xlibris Corporation, 2009
Miller, Joseph C. "Nzinga of Matamba in a New

Perspective", *The Journal of African History*, vol. 16, no. 2, 1975, 201–216

Stapleton, T. J. Njinga Mbande, Queen of Ndongo and Matamba (ca. 1583–1663), *The Encyclopedia of War*, www.onlinelibrary.wiley.com/doi/10.1002/9781444338232.wbeow451/references. Accessed 21 May, 2017

Thornton, John K. "Legitimacy and Political Power: Queen Njinga, 1624–1663", *The Journal of African History*, vol. 32, no. 1, 1991, 25–40, www.jstor.org/stable/182577

www.blogs.harvard.edu/preserving/2013/11/18/the-enigmatic-queen-nzinga-of-ndongo. Accessed 21 May, 2017

UNESCO. "Njinga Mbandi: Queen of Ndongo and Matamba", www.unesdoc.unesco.org/ages/0023/002301/230103E.pdf. Accessed 21 May, 2017

Virginia Hall (1906–1982)

Lineberry, Cate. "WANTED: The Limping Lady", *Smithsonian.com*, 1 February 2007, www.smithsonianmag.com/history/wanted-the-limping-lady-146541513/. Accessed 13 May, 2017

Mawer, Simon. "Special Agents: The Women of SOE", *The Paris Review*, 21 May 2012

Pearson, Judith L. *The Wolves at the Door: The True Story of America's Greatest Female Spy*, Diversion Books, 2014

www.theparisreview.org/blog/2012/05/21/special-agents-the-women-of-soe. Accessed 13 May, 2017

www.cia.gov/news-information/featured-story-archive/2007-featured-story-archive/the-people-of-the-cia.html. Accessed 13 May, 2017

www.cia.gov/news-information/featured-story-archive/2015-featured-story-archive/virginia-hall-the-courage-and-daring-of-the-limping-lady.html. Accessed 13 May, 2017

Ranavalona I (1778–1861)

Berg, Gerald M. "Writing Ideology: Ranavalona, the Ancestral Bureaucrat", *History in Africa*, vol. 22, 1995, 73–92, www.jstor.org/stable/3171909

Brown, Mervyn. "Ranavalona I and the Missionaries, 1828-1840", *Omaly sy Anio 6*, 1977, 107–39. www.madarevues.recherches.gov.mg/IMG/pdf/omaly5-6_9_.pdf. Accessed 17 May, 2017

Ellis, William and Freeman, J.J. *History of Madagascar. Comprising also the progress of the Christian mission established in 1818, and an authentic account of the persecution and recent martyrdom of the native Christians*, Fisher, Son & Co, 1838

Jackson, Guida M. *Women Leaders of Africa, Asia, Middle East, and Pacific: A Biographical Reference*, Xlibris Corporation, 2009

Kamhi, Alison. "Perceptions of Ranavalona I: A Malagasy Historic Figure as a Thematic Symbol of Malagasy Attitudes Toward History", *Stanford Undergraduate Research Journal*, May 2002, 29–32

Klein, Martin A. "Campbell, Gwyn—An Economic History of Imperial Madagascar, 1750–1895: The Rise and Fall of an Island Empire", *Histoire sociale/Social History* 39.78, 2006

Middleton, John. *World monarchies and dynasties*, Routledge, 2015

Pfeiffer, Ida. *The last travels of Ida Pfeiffer : inclusive of a visit to Madagascar, with a biographical memoir of the author*, Harper & Brothers, 1861

Skeie, Karina Hestad. *Building God's Kingdom: Norwegian Missionaries in Highland Madagascar 1866–1903*, Vol. 42. Brill, 2012

Tarenorerer (c.1800–1831)

Boyce, James. *Van Diemen's Land: A History*, Black Inc, 2010

Matson-Green, Vicki maikutena. 'Tarenorerer', *Australian Dictionary of Biography*, www.adb.anu.edu.au/biography/tarenorerer-13212. Accessed 15 May, 2017

Merry, Kay, Stephen Murray-smith, and Iain Stuart. "The cross-cultural relationships between the sealers and the Tasmanian Aboriginal women at Bass Strait and Kangaroo Island in the early nineteenth century", *Journal of Australian Studies* 66, 2000, 73–84

www.pandora.nla.gov.au/pan/78644/20071105-1315/www.200australianwomen.com/names/011.html. Accessed 15 May, 2017

THE WARRIORS

The Trung Sisters (c. AD 12–43)

Logan, William Stewart. *Hanoi: Biography of a city*, UNSW Press, 2000

Miksic, John N, and Geok Yian Goh. *Ancient Southeast Asia*, Taylor & Francis, 2016

Pelley, Patricia M. *Postcolonial Vietnam: New histories of the national past*, Duke University Press, 2002

Taylor, Keith Weller. "The Trung Sisters in the Literature of Later Centuries", *Southeast Asia: past and present*, ed. SarDesai, Damodar Ramaji, Westview Press, 2012

Werner, Jayne, John K. Whitmore, and George Dutton, eds. *Sources of Vietnamese tradition*, Columbia University Press, 2012

Womack, Sarah. "The Remakings of a Legend: Women and Patriotism in the Hagiography of the Tru'ng Sisters", *Crossroads: An Interdisciplinary Journal of Southeast Asian Studies*, vol. 9, no. 2, 1995, 31–50, www.jstor.org/stable/40860533

Tomyris (c. 5th century BC)

Herodotus, *The History*, trans. George Rawlinson, Dutton & Co, 1862

Shepherd, R trans. *Polyænus's Stratagems of War*, printed for George Nicol, 1793

West, Barbara A. *Encyclopedia of the Peoples of Asia and Oceania*, Infobase Publishing, 2010

Weststeijn, Johan. "Wine, Women, and Revenge in Near Eastern Historiography: The Tales of Tomyris, Judith, Zenobia, and Jalila", *Journal of Near Eastern Studies* 75.1, 2016, 91–107

Khawlah bint al-Azwar (7th century AD)

al-Faẓl 'Izzatī, Abū, and A. Ezzati. *The spread of Islam: The contributing factors*, ICAS Press, 2002

Bachay, Judith Barr, and Rául Fernández-Calienes, eds. *Women Moving Forward Volume Two: An Intersectional Lens for*

a Tapestry of Diverse Voices. Vol. 2, Cambridge Scholars Publishing, 2010
Heath, Jennifer. *The Scimitar and the veil: Extraordinary women of Islam*, Paulist Press, 2004
Talhami, Ghada. *Historical dictionary of women in the Middle East and North Africa*, Scarecrow Press, 2012

Mochizuki Chiyome (c. 16th century AD)
Cummins, Antony. *In Search of the Ninja: The Historical Truth of Ninjutsu*, The History Press, 2012
Hayes, Stephen. *Legacy of the Night Warrior*, Black Belt Communications, 1984
Hayes, Stephen K. *Ninja and Their Secret Fighting Art*, Tuttle Publishing, 2011
Turnbull, Stephen. *Ninja AD 1460–1650*, Bloomsbury Publishing, 2012
Warner, Jennifer. *Ninja Warrior: 10 Ninjas That Changed History, Golgotha Press*, 2016
Yoda, Hiroko and Alt, Matt. *Ninja Attack!: True Tales of Assassins, Samurai, and Outlaws*, Tuttle Shokai Inc, 2012

Qiu Jin (1875–1907)
Edwards, Louise P. Gender, *Politics, and Democracy: Women's Suffrage in China*, Stanford University Press, 2008
Edwards, Louise. *Women Warriors and Wartime Spies of China*, Cambridge University Press, 2016
Fan, Hong. *Footbinding, feminism, and freedom: the liberation of women's bodies in modern China*, Vol. 1, Psychology Press, 1997
Finnane, Antonia. *Changing clothes in China: Fashion, history, nation*, Columbia University Press, 2008
Yan, Haiping. *Chinese women writers and the feminist imagination*, 1905-1948, Routledge, 2006
Wang, Zheng. *Women in the Chinese enlightenment: Oral and textual histories*, University of California Press, 1999

Edith Margaret Garrud (1872–1971)
Godfrey, Emelyne. *Femininity, Crime and Self-Defence in Victorian Literature and Society: From Dagger-Fans to Suffragettes*, Springer, 2012
Williams, Jean. *A Contemporary History of Women's Sport, Part One: Sporting Women, 1850-1960*, Vol. 3, Routledge, 2014
Ruz, Camila and Parkinson, Justin, "'Suffrajitsu': How the suffragettes fought back using martial arts", *BBC News*, www.bbc.co.uk/news/magazine-34425615. Accessed 5 July, 2017
Wolf, Tony and Katherine. *Edith Garrud: The Suffragette Who Knew Jujutsu*, Lulu Press Inc, 2013

Ching Shih (1775–1844)
Banerji, Urvija, "The Chinese Female Pirate Who Commanded 80,000 Outlaws", *Atlas Obscura*, www.atlasobscura.com/articles/the-chinese-female-pirate-who-commanded-80000-outlaws. Accessed 5 July, 2017
Pennell, C. Richard, ed. *Bandits at sea: A pirates reader*, NYU Press, 2001
Zurndorfer, Harriet T. "Journal of the Economic and Social History of the Orient", *Journal of the Economic and Social History of the Orient*, vol. 33, no. 2, 1990, 234–36, www.jstor.org/stable/3632229

Zenobia (AD 240–unknown)
Mark, Joshua J. "Zenobia", *Ancient History Encyclopedia*, 14 September 2014, www.ancient.eu/zenobia. Accessed 3 July, 2017
Stoneman, Richard. *Palmyra and its Empire: Zenobia's revolt against Rome*, University of Michigan Press, 1994
Winsbury, Rex. *Zenobia of Palmyra: history, myth and the neo-classical imagination*, Duckworth, 2010

Amina of Zazzau (c. 14th century)
Awe, Bolanle. *Nigerian women in historical perspective*, Bookcraft, 1992
Coles, Catherine M., and Beverly Mack, eds. *Hausa women in the twentieth century*, University of Wisconsin Press, 1991
Madden, Annette. *In Her Footsteps: 101 Remarkable Black Women from the Queen of Sheba to Queen Latifah*, Conari Press, 2000
Martin. J.P. *African Empires: Your Guide to the Historical Record of Africa* Vol 2, Trafford Publishing, 2017
Sheldon, Kathleen. *Historical dictionary of women in Sub-Saharan Africa*, Rowman & Littlefield, 2016

THE RULERS

Hatshepsut (c.1508 BC–c.1458 BC)
Fletcher, J. *The Story of Egypt*, Hodder, 2016
Izadi, Elahe. "A new discovery sheds light on ancient Egypt's most successful female pharoh", *Washington Post*, 23 April 2016
Wilson, Elizabeth B. "The Queen Who Would Be King", *Smithsonian Magazine*, September 2006, www.smithsonianmag.com/history/the-queen-who-would-be-king-130328511. Accessed 8 June, 2017
www.ngm.nationalgeographic.com/2009/04/hatshepsut/brown-text/4. Accessed 8 June, 2017

Toregene Kathun (unknown–c.1241)
Davis-Kimball, Jeannine. "Katuns: The Mongolian Queens of the Genghis Khanite", *Ancient Queens: Archaeological Explorations 5*, 2003, 151
Weatherford, Jack. *The secret history of the Mongol queens: how the daughters of Genghis Khan rescued his empire*, Broadway Books, 2011
Weatherford, J. McIver. *Genghis Khan and the making of the modern world*, Broadway Books, 2004

Brunhilda of Austrasia (c. AD 543 – AD 613)
Bauer, Susan Wise. *The history of the medieval world: From the conversion of Constantine to the first crusade*, WW Norton & Company, 2010
Dahmus, Joseph Henry. *Seven medieval queens*, Doubleday, 1972
Fredegar, Fredegarii *Chronicorum Liber Quartus*

cum Continuationibus, trans. JM Wallace www.rebelwomenembroidery.wordpress.com/2016/07/02/brunhilda-c-543-613-merovingian-austrasia. Accessed 3 June, 2017

Gregory of Tours, *History of the Franks*, trans. Ernest Brehaut (extended selections), Records of Civilization 2, Columbia University Press, 1916

www.britannica.com/biography/Brunhild-queen-of-Austrasia. Accessed 3 June, 2017

Zoë Porphyrogenita (c. AD 978 – AD 1050)

Connor, Carolyn L. *Women of Byzantium*, Yale University Press, 2004

Garland, Lynda. *Byzantine Empresses: Women and Power in Byzantium AD 527–1204*, Routledge, 2002

Panas, Marios, et al. "The Byzantine Empress Zoe Porphyrogenita and the quest for eternal youth", *Journal of cosmetic dermatology* 11.3, 2012, 245–8

Catherine de Medici (1519–1589)

Foreman, Amanda. "Catherine the Great?", the *Observer*, 11 January 2004

Frieda, Leonie. *Catherine de Medici: A biography*, Hachette UK, 2011

Gordetsky, Jennifer, Ronald Rabinowitz, and Jeanne O'Brien. "The 'infertility' of Catherine de Medici and its influence on 16th century France", *Canadian Journal of Urology* 16.2, 2009, 4585

Knecht, Robert Jean. *Catherine De'Medici*, Routledge, 2014

Knecht, Robert. *The Valois: Kings of France 1328–1589*, A&C Black, 2007

Anacaona (c.1474–c.1503)

Accilien, Cécile, Jessica Adams, and Elmide Méléance. *Revolutionary Freedoms: A History of Survival, Strength and Imagination in Haiti*, Educa Vision Inc., 2006

Monbiot, George. "The Holocaust We Will Not See", 11 January 2010, www.monbiot.com/2010/01/11/the-holocaust-we-will-not-see. Accessed 1 June, 2017

Poole, Robert M. "What Became of the Taíno?", *Smithsonian Magazine*, October 2011, www.smithsonianmag.com/people-places/what-became-of-the-taino-73824867/?all. Accessed 1 June, 2017

Rodriguez, Junius P., ed. *Encyclopedia of slave resistance and rebellion*, Vol. 2. Greenwood Publishing Group, 2007

Seaman, Rebecca M., ed. *Conflict in the Early Americas: An Encyclopedia of the Spanish Empire's Aztec, Incan, and Mayan Conquests: An Encyclopedia of the Spanish Empire's Aztec, Incan, and Mayan Conquests*, ABC-CLIO, 2013

Saunders, Nicholas J. *The peoples of the Caribbean: An encyclopedia of archeology and traditional culture*, ABC-CLIO, 2005

Catherine the Great (1729–1796)

Massie, Robert K. *Catherine the Great: portrait of a woman*, Random House Incorporated, 2011

Meehan-Waters, Brenda. "Catherine the Great and the problem of female rule", *The Russian Review* 34.3, 1975, 293–307

Raeff, Marc. *Catherine the Great: a profile*, Springer, 1972

Jadwiga of Poland (1373/4–1399)

Frost, Robert. *The Making of the Polish-Lithuanian Union 1385-1569*, Volume 1, OUP Oxford, 2015

Gromada, Thaddeus V. "Oscar Halecki's Vision of Saint Jadwiga of Anjou", *The Polish Review*, vol. 44, no. 4, 1999, 433–7, www.jstor.org/stable/25779153

Jackson, Guida M., ed. *Women Leaders of Europe and the Western Hemisphere: A Biographical Reference*, Xlibris Corporation, 2009

Knoll, Paul W. "Jadwiga and Education", *The Polish Review* 44.4, 1999, 419–32

Parsons, John C., ed. *Medieval queenship*, Macmillan, 1997

Schaus, Margaret C., ed. *Women and gender in medieval Europe: an encyclopedia*, Routledge, 2006

Isabella of Castile (1451–1504)

Downey, Kirstin. *Isabella: The Warrior Queen*, Anchor, 2015

Tremlett, Giles. *Isabella of Castile: Europe's First Great Queen*, Bloomsbury Publishing, 2017

Weissberger, Barbara F. *Isabel Rules: Constructing Queenship, Wielding Power*, University of Minnesota Press, 2004

Seondeok of Silla (ruled AD 632–647)

Cartwright, M. "Queen Seondeok. Ancient History Encyclopedia", 2016, October 14, www.ancient.eu/Queen_Seondeok. Accessed 17 June, 2017

Hwang, Kyung Moon. A *history of Korea*, Palgrave Macmillan, 2016

Lee, Bae-Yong. *Women in Korean History*, Ewha Womans University Press, 2008

Nelson, Sarah M. "The Queens of Silla: Power and Connections to the Spirit World", *Ancient Queens, Archaeological Explorations*, AltaMira Press, 2003, 77–92

Eleanor of Aquitaine (c.1122/1124–1204)

Weir, Alison. *Eleanor of Aquitaine: by the wrath of God, Queen of England*, Random House, 2008

Wheeler, Bonnie, and John C. Parsons, eds. *Eleanor of Aquitaine: lord and lady*, Springer, 2016

Seward, Desmond. *Eleanor of Aquitaine: the mother queen of the middle ages*, Pegasus, reprint edition, 1978/2017

Sammu-ramat (c. 9th century BC)

Budin, Stephanie Lynn, and Jean MacIntosh Turfa, eds. *Women in Antiquity: Real Women Across the Ancient World*, Routledge, 2016

Gera, Deborah Levine. *Warrior women: the anonymous Tractatus de mulieribus*, Vol. 162. Brill, 1997

Mark, Joshua J. "Sammu-Ramat and Semiramis: The Inspiration and the Myth", *Ancient History Encyclopedia*, 16 September 2014. Accessed 11 June, 2017

THE ACTIVISTS

Sylvia Rivera (1952–2002)

Bronski, Michael. "Sylvia Rivera: 1951-2002", *Z Magazine*, 1 April 2012

Feinberg, Leslie, interview with Sylvia Rivera, *Workers World*, 1998, www.workers.org/ww/1998/sylvia0702.php. Accessed 28 May, 2017

Gan, Jessi. "Still at the back of the bus": Sylvia Rivera's struggle", *CENTRO: Journal of the Center for Puerto Rican Studies* 19.1, 2007, 124–40

Rivera, Sylvia. "Sylvia Rivera's Talk at LGMNY, June 2001 Lesbian and Gay Community Services Center, New York City", *Centro Journal* 19.1, 2007

Wilchins, Riki, "A Woman for Her Time", *The Village Voice*, 26 February 2002

Concepción Picciotto (1936–2016)

Austermuhle, Martin, "DCist Interview: Concepción Picciotto", *DCist.com*, www.dcist.com/2005/08/dcist_interview.php. Accessed 28 May, 2017

Gibson, Caitlin, "Concepción Picciotto, who held vigil outside the White House for decades, dies", *Washington Post*, 25 January 2016

Gibson, Caitlin, "Connie Picciotto has kept vigil near the White House for 32 years. Why, and at what cost?", *Washington Post*, 5 February 2013

Gibson, Caitlin, "Pennsylvania Ave. activist Concepción Picciotto's vigil lives on after her death – with some changes", *Washington Post*, 1 March 2016

Peterson, Kierran, "The story behind Concepción Picciotto, Washington's most resolute protester", *PRI's The World*, 27 January 2016, www.pri.org/stories/2016-01-27/who-was-concepción-picciotto-washington-dcs-most-resolute-protester. Accessed 28 May, 2017

Roberts, Sam, "Concepción Picciotto, who kept vigil by White House for three decades, dies", *The New York Times*, 27 January 2016

The Mirabel Sisters (1920s/30s–1960)

Brown, Isabel Zakrzewski. *Culture and customs of the Dominican Republic*, Greenwood Publishing Group, 1999

Manley, Elizabeth. "Intimate Violations: Women and the 'Ajusticiamiento' of Dictator Rafael Trujillo, 1944—1961", *The Americas*, vol. 69, no. 1, 2012, 61–94, www.jstor.org/stable/23270071

Robinson, Nancy P. "Origins of the International Day for the Elimination of Violence against Women: The Caribbean Contribution", *Caribbean Studies*, vol. 34, no. 2, 2006, 141–61, www.jstor.org/stable/25613539

Robinson, Nancy. "Women's Political Participation in the Dominican Republic: The Case of the Mirabal Sisters", *Caribbean Quarterly*, vol. 52, no. 2/3, 2006, 172–83, www.jstor.org/stable/40654568

Rohter, Larry. "The Three Sisters, Avenged: A Dominican Drama", *The New York Times*, 15 February 1997

Tompkins, Cynthia, and David William Foster, eds. *Notable Twentieth-century Latin American Women: A Biographical Dictionary*, Greenwood Publishing Group, 2001

"Mirabal Sisters", *Women in World History: A Biographical Encyclopedia*, 2002, www.encyclopedia.com/women/encyclopedias-almanacs-transcripts-and-maps/mirabal-sisters. Accessed 21 May, 2017

www.un.org/womenwatch/daw/news/vawd.html. Accessed 21 May, 2017

Lillian Ngoyi (1911–1980)

Daymond, Margaret J., ed. *Women writing Africa: The southern region*. Vol. 1, Feminist Press at CUNY, 2003

Gasa, Nomboniso, ed. *Women in South African History: They remove boulders and cross rivers*, HSRC Press, 2007

Mandela, Nelson, spoken address announcing the ANC election victory, 2 May 1994, www.mandela.gov.za/mandela_speeches/1994/940502_anc.htm. Accessed 29 May, 2017

"Lillian Ngoyi", *Encyclopedia.com*, 26 August 2017

www.sahistory.org.za/topic/womens-charter. Accessed 29 May, 2017

www.sahistory.org.za/article/women039s-resistance-against-pass-laws. Accessed 29 May, 2017

Jayaben Desai (1933–2010)

Bell, Bethan and Mahmood, Shabnam, "Grunwich dispute: What did the 'strikers in saris' achieve?", *BBC News*, 10 September 2016, www.bbc.co.uk/news/uk-england-london-37244466. Accessed 30 May, 2017

Dromey, Jack. "Jayaben Desai obituary", the *Guardian*, 28 December 2010

Serpell, Nick, "Been and gone: Tom Walkinshaw, Chuck Jordan and others", *BBC News*, 5 January 2011, www.bbc.co.uk/news/magazine-12110810. Accessed 30 May, 2017

University of Birmingham, Centre for Contemporary Cultural Studies. *The empire strikes back: race and racism in 70s Britain*, Hutchinson Educational, 1982

www.striking-women.org/module/striking-out/grunwick-dispute. Accessed 30 May, 2017

Nazaria Lagos (1851–1945)

Einolf, Christopher J. *America in the Philippines, 1899-1902: The first torture scandal*, Springer, 2016

Quirino, Carlos. *Who's who in Philippine History*, Tahanan Books, 1995

Piccio, Belle, "The Florence Nightingale of Panay Island", *Choose Philippines*, www.choosephilippines.com/specials/people/1515/florence-nightingale-panay. Accessed 5 June, 2017

Soriano, Rafaelita Hilario. *Women in the Philippine Revolution*, RH Soriano, 1995

Tucker, Spencer, ed. *The encyclopedia of the Spanish-American and Philippine-American wars: a political, social, and military history*, Vol. 1, ABC-CLIO, 2009

Mary Ann McCracken (1770–1866)

Metscher, Priscilla. "Mary Ann McCracken: A Critical

Ulsterwoman within the Context of her Times", *Études irlandaises* 14.2, 1989, 143–58
"McCracken, Mary Ann (1770–1866)", *Women in World History: A Biographical Encyclopedia*, www.encyclopedia.com/women/encyclopedias-almanacs-transcripts-and-maps/mccracken-mary-ann-1770-1866. Accessed 29 May, 2017
www.newsletter.co.uk/news/businesswoman-campaigner-the-remarkable-mary-ann-mccracken-1-7492139. Accessed 29 May, 2017

THE REFORMERS

The Radium Girls (early 20th century – 1930s)

Blum, Deborah. "A Dazzle in the Bones", *Wired*, 26 March 2011
Moore, Kate. "The forgotten factory girls killed by radioactive poisoning", the *Telegraph*, 14 June 2016
Moore, Kate. "The Forgotten Story of the Radium Girls, Whose Deaths Saved Thousands of Workers' Lives", *Buzzfeed*, 5 May 2017, www.buzzfeed.com/authorkatemoore/the-light-that-does-not-lie?utm_term=.eqNo91YRG#.amgEpKVza. Accessed 13 May, 2017
Zhang, Sarah. "The Girls with Radioactive Bones", *The Atlantic*, 1 March 2017
www.lgrossman.com/pics/radium. Accessed 13 May, 2017

Zitkala-Ša (1876–1938)

Davidson, Cathy N., and Ada Norris, eds. *American Indian Stories, Legends, and Other Writings*, Penguin, 2003
Hoefel, Roseanne. "Zitkala-Ša: A Biography", *The Online Archive of Nineteenth-Century U.S. Women's Writings*, ed. Glynis Carr, posted Winter 1999
Lewandowski, Tadeusz. *Red Bird, Red Power: The Life and Legacy of Zitkala-Ša*, Vol. 67, University of Oklahoma Press, 2016
Zitkala-Ša [aka Gertrude Simmons Bonnin], *American Indian Stories*, Washington: Hayworth Publishing House, 1921

Ruth Simpson (1926–2008)

Simpson, Ruth. *From the closet to the courts: The lesbian transition*, Take Root Media, 2007
Tobin, Kay, and Randy Wicker. *The gay crusaders*, Arno Press, 1975
Woo, Elaine. "Ruth Simpson Obituary: Writer, leader in gay liberation movement", *LA Times*, 17 May 2008

Shirley Chisholm (1924–2005)

Barron, James. "Shirley Chisholm, 'Unbossed' Pioneer in Congress, Is Dead at 80", *The New York Times*, 3 January 2005
Kazmi, Laila and Hegg, Stephen. "What former presidential candidate Shirley Chisholm said about facing gender discrimination", *The Rundown*, 13 September 2016, www.pbs.org/newshour/rundown/what-former-presidential-candidate-shirley-chisholm-said-about-facing-gender-discrimination/. Accessed 1 July, 2017
Landers, Jackson. "When Shirley Chisholm Ran for President, Few Would Say: 'I'm With Her'", *Smithsonian.com*, 25 April 2016, www.smithsonianmag.com/smithsonian-institution/when-shirley-chisholm-ran-for-president-few-would-say-im-with-her-180958699/. Accessed 1 July, 2017
Nichols, John. "Shirley Chisholm Made the Democratic Party of Today Possible", *The Nation*, 6 June 2016, www.thenation.com/article/shirley-chisholm-made-the-democratic-party-of-today-possible/. Accessed 1 July, 2017
Vaidyanathan, Raijini. "Before Hillary Clinton, there was Shirley Chisholm", *BBC News*, 26 January 2016, www.bbc.co.uk/news/magazine-35057641. Accessed 1 July, 2017

Jeanette Rankin (1880–1973)

O'Brien, Mary Barmeyer. *Jeannette Rankin: Bright Star in the Big Sky*, TwoDot Books, 2015
Smith, Norma. *Jeannette Rankin, America's Conscience*, Montana Historical Society, 2002
Walbert, Kate. "Has anything changed for female politicians?", *The New Yorker*, 16 August 2016
Zeitz, Josh. "The Congresswoman Who Paved the Way for Hillary Clinton", *Politico Magazine*, 2 November 2016, www.politico.com/magazine/story/2016/11/the-congresswoman-who-paved-the-way-for-hillary-clinton-214413. Accessed 12 June, 2017
History, Art & Archives, United States House of Representatives, Jeannette Rankin Biography, www.history.house.gov/People/Listing/R/RANKIN,-Jeannette-(R000055)/#biography. Accessed 12 June, 2017

Ida B. Wells (1862–1931)

McMurry, Linda O. *To keep the waters troubled: The life of Ida B. Wells*, Oxford University Press on Demand, 2000
Wells-Barnett, Ida B. "Southern Horrors: Lynch Law in All Its Phases, 1892", *Wells-Barnett, On Lynchings*, 1991, 25–54
Wells, Ida B. *Crusade for justice: The autobiography of Ida B. Wells*, University of Chicago Press, 2013
www.britannica.com/biography/Ida-B-Wells-Barnett#ref138160. Accessed 12 June, 2017
www.biography.com/people/ida-b-wells-9527635. Accessed 12 June, 2017

Sojourner Truth (c.1797–1883)

Truth, Sojourner. *Narrative of Sojourner Truth*, J. B. Yerrinton and Son, Printers, 1850
Truth, Sojourner, "A life, a symbol", *New York*: WW Norton 226, 1996, 229–32
Washington, Margaret. *Sojourner Truth's America*, University of Illinois Press, 2011

Allegra Lockstadt

Allegra Lockstadt was born in Canada, raised in the Southeastern United States, and currently resides in the Minneapolis, Minnesota, US. She currently works as freelance illustrator and designer. To see more of Allegra's work visit **www.allegralockstadt.com**

Sara Netherway

Sara Netherway is an illustrator from the Isle of Wight. Originally trained in fine art, she enjoys creating images with rich textures and detail. To see more of Sara's work visit **www.saranetherway.co.uk**

Lauren Simkin Berke

Lauren Simkin Berke is an American artist and illustrator based in Brooklyn, NY. Working in ink on paper, Lauren draws for clients such as *The New York Times*, *Smithsonian* magazine, Simon & Schuster publishers, and Rémy Martin.
www.simkinberke.com

Hannah Berman

Hannah Berman lives and works in Oakland, California. She loves to travel, collect bird nests and antiques, and is inspired by candy wrappers, Paint-By Numbers kits, and Islamic miniatures.

María Hergueta

María Hergueta is a freelance illustrator from a small village in north Spain. She has been working as an illustrator for five years now and her work has been published in different publishing houses and magazines such as Oxford University Press, Penguin Books and the *New York Times*.

She currently lives between Barcelona and the Swedish countryside.

Miriam Castillo

Miriam Castillo is an illustrator based in Brooklyn and Mexico. Her whimsical hand-drawn illustrations explore the intersection in between yoga, spirituality and nature. For more of her world, visit **www.miriamcastillo.com**

Marcela Quiroz

Marcela works as an illustrator for publishing projects and print media. Her day is divided between books and pencils, searching for new words, memorizing them, and writing them over and over again until they become drawings and become part of some of their alphabets of illustrated words.

www.do-re-mi.co

Shreyas Krishnan

Shreyas is an illustrator-designer from Chennai, India. She is curious about the ways in which art, design and gender intersect. Through drawing and writing, she tries to understand how, why and what we remember.

www.shreyasrkrishnan.com

Laura Inksetter

Laura Inksetter is an artist and illustrator from Ottawa, Ontario, Canada. Her work is inspired by history, folklore, and the natural world. She has a master's degree in medieval history.

Tanya Heidrich

Tanya is a Swiss, American and German graphic designer and illustrator who designs in colour, and illustrates in black and white drawing inspiration from patterns and details in everyday life.

www.tanyaheidri.ch

W T Frick

Winnie T Frick is a comic artist and illustrator currently based in Brooklyn. Her interests include, cross-hatching, architecture, and dopple-gangers. Her illustrations and webcomics can be found on **www.ipsumlorum.com**

Hélène Baum

Hélène Baum is a Berlin-based illustrator. “There are no lines in nature, only areas of colour, one against another” (Manet). This principle guides her work and life. With her diverse cultural background and much traveling, she creates a cosmic space through which humour, idealism and elements from diferent cultures coexist in vibrant images.

Grace Helmer

Grace Helmer is a Brighton-born, London-based illustrator. She has put her paintbrushes to work for a range of clients, including Apple, Google, HarvardX and *Marie Claire*.
www.gracehelmer.co.uk

The New Historia

In creating this series, the author and publisher have worked with Gina Luria Walker, Professor of Women's Studies at The New School, New York City, and Director of The New Historia, carefully building, curating and editing the list of 48 women within this book to ensure that we uncovered as many lost female histories as possible. The New Historia's ongoing work is dedicated to the discovery, recovery, and authoritative reclamation of women of the past through time and around the globe, and honour earlier women by telling their stories and sharing their strategies that inspire us to be sturdy and brave. In them we find our foremothers, transforming and remaking our ideas about history and ourselves.

"It is imperative that we galvanize what we know so that women's legacy is acknowledged as essential to the continuum of human enlightenment. Activating what we know will also keep us from making contemporary women invisible — waiting to be brought to life 50 or 100 years from now." Gina Luria Walker, The New Historia

www.thenewhistoria.com

Index

This book is for my mother and for all the other women in my life, but mainly my mother. Thank you for putting up with me.

Forgotten Women would not have existed without publishing supremo Romilly Morgan, who sought me out for a coffee and dared me to think about writing a book – and then commissioned me to write a series. I would also like to thank the team at Octopus, The New Historia, and all the illustrators from Women Who Draw who brought these women to life in such vivid colour. Special thanks go to Daniel Johnson and my agent Emma Paterson of Rogers, Coleridge & White.

Zing Tsjeng

The Publisher would like to thank the entire team involved in curating the list of women featured in *Forgotten Women: The Leaders*, and in particular would like to praise The New Historia centre's ongoing work in rediscovering women's contributions throughout history.

The Publisher would also like to thank Mala Sanghera-Warren and Natasha Borkowski for their assistance in researching this book.